I Am Not Your ATM

A Practical Plan For Teaching Your Teen To Manage Money

Rachel Murphy

Murphy Solutions, LLC

https://rachelmurphycoaching.com
ISBN: 978-1-7376214-1-6

Book Design by Honoray Joseph

If you had told me almost twenty years ago that I would one day write a book on finance, I would have laughed at you. But our biggest weaknesses have a way of becoming our greatest strengths if we let them. I hope our story inspires you to realize that you can make a difference in your teen's life. You can give them an amazing start as they launch out into the world!

Looking forward,

Rachel

Is This Book for You?

I don't want to waste your time. I don't believe every parent needs this book, but I do want to help those that do. So, if you fall into one of the categories below, feel free to put this book down and go about your day. We can still be friends, though, right?

- If you have already been teaching your teens about finances and feel confident in their ability to handle the adult world, you don't need this book.

- If you don't spend money at all on your kids (you never buy them clothes [not even thrift store ones] or take them out to eat, pay for any of their activities, or buy them anything), this book is not for you.

- If your teen has a job, pays all their own expenses, and can handle savings and delayed gratification, this may not be the book for you.

- If you don't want to expend any effort and just want to hope it will all work out in the future, this definitely is not the book for you.

However...

- If you feel like your teen's hand is always outstretched asking for funds and you sometimes feel like his or her personal ATM, this is for you.

- If you feel like your teen just doesn't grasp the value of the dollar and wastes money more than you think he or she should, keep reading.

- If you spend good money on buying items your child needs only to find them outgrown, never worn, in their closet, I'm your girl.

This has to be a priority. It will never be a good time to start. You just have to make time. Anything new or different feels a little scary. It's okay. In just a few months, you will look back and be glad you started.

Table of Contents

Foreword

How do you succeed in life? Years ago I studied many formulas to enhance your opportunity for success. One claimed that you must have passion for something, then practice that effort, and finally achieve great performance. This is true, but it must be preceded by the establishment of high standards, distinct planning and resolute execution.

We have known the Murphys personally for almost twenty years and seen them work their way through many financial challenges and come out on the other side. The proof of the effectiveness of this teaching is reflected in the mature attitude of their children. Now Rachel has documented their personal journey for the benefit of all. Their testimony will give you a unique jumpstart as you prepare your young ones to become confident adults, giving a full measure and making a meaningful contribution to society.

Lt. Col. Jack O'Brien

Chapter One
What Happened to the Fairy Tale?

Money is a terrible master, but an excellent servant.
—P. T. Barnum

Once upon a time there lived a senior in college that was a long-haired rocker wannabe. He met an equally long-haired college sophomore. They would spend hours and hours planning their lives and talking about how great life was going to be. They wanted to have a house and a family and work with young people. They had lots of big dreams for the future. Like most young couples, they began their marriage full of positivity and ready to change the world. But less than ten years later their dreams had all seemingly slipped out of their grasp.

Let's Start a Business

A few years into our marriage, we started our own business. Keith, my husband, is a self-proclaimed nerd. As a kid he was so excited when his family purchased a Commodore 64 - what would be considered painfully slow to us now was cutting edge back then. That began his love affair with computers. In college, he made money building computers for people, and he also had a job at the help desk in the computer lab on campus.

When the internet was just becoming popular for the average person, we started a local internet service provider. Remember those days when you had to unplug the cable from your phone and plug it into the modem? Your modem would then dial out to connect to the internet making the most annoying sound as it connected. More and more people were getting personal computers and wanting to surf the web. You would try to call someone, and their line would be constantly busy. You would say, "I can't get through. Someone is on the internet." Back then hardly anyone had cell phones, so not only could you not reach people when they weren't at home, but also it became increasingly difficult to reach them when they were home.

In order to use a landline phone to connect to the internet, a person had to sign up and pay for a monthly service, kind of a precursor to what the big companies like AT&T and Mediacom do now. Back then there were a few big companies like AOL and lots of small local companies. Our company, PowerHouse Communications, provided local dial-up internet service. Customers would dial into our number to connect. Man, that was such a different world, it makes us sound so old! I would like to think that maybe I'm not old; it's just that progress happened so fast.

Keith had the technical know-how, but neither of us knew how to run a business. You can probably imagine how things turned out. A year in and we were starting to get into financial trouble. Keith had to find another job to pay the bills. He couldn't find work in our area, so we moved five hours away to Atlanta and continued to work our business remotely. Lonely, we would often load up our toddler and drive home on the weekends. Money was tight, and looking back we probably shouldn't have been driving home so often.

One weekend found us making the trek back to Florida. We were in Alabama about an hour away and needed gas. There was an old mom-and-pop gas station in Alabama right on the border of Alabama and Florida. When Keith went to pay, they wouldn't take his check because it was an out-of-state check. We had barely any money in the bank, but we were supposed to be getting paid in a couple of days. Back then, if you wrote a check, the money wouldn't be taken out of your account immediately. You normally had a few days until it was transferred to the other bank. Forced to pay with our debit card, we were so stressed out knowing that buying that gas was probably going to start a chain reaction and cause something else to bounce.

I don't know if you have ever found yourself in a situation like that, worrying about a credit card being declined, trying to juggle bills that need to get paid. It puts so much stress on you and your relationships. But how in the world did we get there?

Normal Kids

We both grew up as normal middle-class kids. Our parents, on the other hand, had very interesting childhoods. My dad's father worked on ranches taking care of livestock, planting and harvesting crops, and taking care of the gardens. My dad went to work at a young age to help his family. He worked hard at collecting, chopping, and hauling wood, hauling water, baling hay, and hunting for his family. At the age of ten or eleven, he drove a tractor pulling a double wagon all the way across the state of Indiana to deliver a load of corn. My dad learned the value and satisfaction of hard work. Having survived both the Great Depression and World War II, his parents feared going without food and were constantly stockpiling. Even though they didn't make much and were considered lower class, they managed to save money.

My mom is the oldest of eighteen(?) I put the question mark there because we aren't really sure about the number of siblings. You can already tell that this story is going to be crazy, can't you? She grew up on the peninsula of Malaysia. Her dad was a businessman and inventor. The Asian culture she was raised in put a high priority on having sons. My grandfather also had several wives, two of them having babies at the same hospital at the same time. Well, her dad had the reproducing part down but ended up with a lot more girls than boys. The girls were not considered important, and several of them were given away. Thirty years later, one of those girls, who had relocated to Sweden, was back in Malaysia for a visit. A friend of my mom's family saw her and told her that she looked just like one of my aunts. That is the story behind how we found my Aunt Peggy. Over the years the family reconnected with several more of my mom's sisters. It's like a soap opera, but we will save those stories for another book.

My mom took a boat across the ocean at the age of eighteen to go to nursing school, where she met my dad. He had enlisted in the Air Force and was stationed in England. He eventually talked her into marrying him after proposing to her three times. (I learned persistence from my dad.)

They moved back to the United States, where my brother and I were born. My mother was a stay-at-home mom until we were in high school. Then she went back into the workforce, got her nursing license, and worked as an RN. After I graduated high school, my parents went on to spend more than twenty years helping people in third-world countries. My parents were both very good with money, though I didn't realize how good until many years later. Even though for most of my childhood we were a one-income family living on an enlisted military income, my parents managed to save and give away a large portion of their income. They were great examples of generosity, frugality, and delayed gratification.

I was pretty good with money. I was already a saver by nature. As a little kid, even my candy was squirreled away and carefully rationed out. My brother would eat all of his and then come begging for me to give him some from my stash.

A very little-known fact about me: when I was in middle school, I was a ventriloquist. I would save up my money to buy courses and dummies. My parents would pay us for a good report card, and I worked at an insurance company filing paperwork for $2 an hour. I had my sights set on the most amazing dummy ever—he could raise his eyebrows, raise one arm, and spit! I would study the ventriloquist catalog like most kids studied the toy catalog.

He cost hundreds of dollars, and I saved a long time to buy him and his home - a shiny black trunk. That was my first really big financial goal. It was a short-lived career, though. I would occasionally do performances for the kids at church, but I was painfully shy back then and had trouble getting up in front of people.

Keith's dad was born to a very young couple. His mother was sixteen when he was born. Much of his dad's childhood was spent living with his paternal grandmother. She would wash other people's clothes and clean the local doctor's office to make enough money to support the two of them. His mom grew up the child of a poor farmer. She lived in a drafty little log cabin that had no running water with her four brothers and sisters and her parents.

Keith's dad also joined the military. After the Vietnam War, he got out of the Air Force, and then he and Keith's mom became teachers. Later on, his dad joined the civil service, and his mom ran her own quilt shop. Keith's parents decided they were going to live differently than they had been raised. They educated themselves by reading financial books and magazines. Money has rules that it operates by, and they made it a point to learn them. That's not to say they didn't make any financial mistakes, but in general they made good financial decisions. And though they probably talked to Keith about money, he doesn't remember any of those lessons.

Keith's first money-making venture was selling chicken eggs. He had various jobs throughout high school. He did laundry for a daycare, washed dishes at a Holiday Inn, and worked at a grocery store. He was more of a spender - a fly-by-the-seat-of-the-pants kind of guy. Most of his income went toward cassettes, then later CDs (the music kind, not the bank kind) and food.

When he was away at college, his parents would put money into his bank account for his needs. Unfortunately, he didn't keep a budget or balance his checkbook. On one trip to the grocery store, he wrote a check for a carton of ice cream, and the check bounced. We now joke about the most expensive ice cream ever, but at that time, it wasn't funny.

We got married fairly young, and the money stress started not long after. It didn't help that our income was so small. The saying, "Two can live cheaper than one," is only true if one goes hungry and the other goes naked. The saver and the spender collided, which led to lots of resentment on both sides. I would be upset because he would blow the budget, and he would be upset because I seemed incapable of having any fun. (I still struggle with that.)

The Crash

Seven years after we married, it all came crashing down. We had owned the business for several years, but we were losing money every month and prolonging the inevitable with credit cards. One of my friends stopped by our home to see us and our little boy. She noticed that we had a rather urgent-looking letter from our credit card company. I told her, "We don't open the yellow ones." What was the point? We had slipped past the point of no return. By the time we sold the company, we had about $50,000 in personal debt and no jobs.

We debated over and over about what we were going to do. We asked many people we respected for advice - almost all of them told us that we needed to declare bankruptcy. The debt was soul-crushing and we had no income. We couldn't sleep at night; the huge looming cloud of debt consumed our thoughts. We went round and round about declaring bankruptcy. One day we would say, "We need to do it," and the next day we would change our minds.

I remember when Keith came home and told me that he had made an appointment with a bankruptcy attorney. There was no relief in hearing that, only a sense of sadness and a feeling of failure. We ended up canceling that appointment because we didn't feel any peace about declaring bankruptcy. If you have ever found yourself in a situation like that, I feel for you. We have no judgment on anyone that has done that, because we understand the pressure.

More Struggles

That decision to dig our way out was one of the hardest decisions we have ever had to make. But once we decided, we knew that it was the right thing for us, and we didn't look back. However, circumstances did not magically change. We sold everything that we possibly could, including Keith's collection of over three hundred music CDs and my ventriloquist dummies. We faced several really tough years. Keith had trouble finding a job. Finally, he found work all the way across the country in California.

Unfortunately, this was not the greatest time to be working in the technology industry; it was the end of the dot com crash. Within nine months he was let go from three different companies as a result of a buyout, a bankruptcy, and finally, a merger. We started off with a six-figure salary, taking a huge pay cut at each new company. After the layoff from the last company, no one was hiring for tech jobs. I had just miscarried our second child right before the layoff. We were emotionally depleted.

The morning of September 11, 2001, we woke up in our hotel room and turned on the television. We had just flown in from a visit to China to see my parents the previous day. Unable to sleep because of jetlag, we watched the plane hit the south tower. We drove to the storage unit where all our belongings were being kept, packed up a moving truck and started the long drive back to Florida from California. It felt like we were living in a really bad science fiction movie. The trip was so surreal. Our country was in turmoil, and once again, so were we.

After that Keith really floundered around for many years. His self-confidence was totally shot, and he became stuck thinking he could never succeed. He worked at low-income jobs for many years, too scared of failure to risk the IT job market again. He ended up driving a taxi for about five years. Many people would have looked at our situation and said that our struggles were the result of bad luck or underemployment, but the most harmful issues were our wrong beliefs about ourselves and our capabilities.

All this time we continued to pay down the debt on a $28K-a-year average annual income. Finally about five years after we committed to paying it off, we were free. Slower and more important than our financial shift came our mindset shift, realizing that all those bad things that happened weren't reflections of what we could accomplish. Those years were so hard, and they lasted longer than necessary. We just didn't have the knowledge and the belief that would enable us to change. We had to get over our regrets, our fears, and our doubts. It was a process, and one that I am still working on to this day.

In 2007 Keith finally got back into the computer industry and began to advance in his field. We slowly began to believe in ourselves and what we could do. Today, we are living a life that we could never have imagined when we were in the depths of discouragement, driving $1,500 cars and feeling trapped by our circumstances.

Let's Do Something Different

Even though our parents had taught or thought they had taught us about money to some degree, we didn't really grasp those lessons. As our kids got older we realized that we didn't want them to go through similar circumstances when they launched out on their own. Sure, they are going to face challenges. However, if they have a strong financial foundation, every challenge doesn't become a money challenge.

One of the main focuses of our family became teaching our kids money management in a realistic, hands-on way. We wanted to introduce concepts and build on them gradually, rather than just letting them figure it out for themselves when they graduated. We wanted our kids to make their financial mistakes where Mom and Dad could help them and it wouldn't be so painful and costly if they messed up. So that's what we did, and it provided so many teachable moments. Now we want to help you and your teen do the same.

I wanted to take a moment to explain the rest of the book to you. Understanding money is not difficult. What is hard is changing thoughts and behaviors. For that reason, I want to take a few chapters to really talk through how most people approach money. In the next chapter we are going to discuss how most people learn about money and the long-term results of that method. Then in chapter three I will share about an important concept that we learned with our children that will help your teen become a better, more confident learner. In chapter four we will talk about long-term goals and what success with money looks like for your teen. Finally in chapter five we will introduce the plan and spend the rest of the book answering questions and helping you implement it. All of these chapters will build upon each other and help you understand the process thoroughly.

Let's get started.

Chapter Two
Are You Okay with Average?

If you don't want average results,
don't do what the average person does.
—Unknown

We realize that while we were taught some financial lessons as young people, a lot of it was theory. There was no practical hands-on training on how to manage money, other than the basics - save some, give some, spend the rest. And that is not a criticism of our parents. They probably taught us the way they were raised, but the financial world changed between their childhood and ours. Most of our parents' generation did not use credit cards when they were young adults. The ability to easily buy on credit has totally transformed the way people handle money. Our parents did not know how to guide us through the changing world of credit, much like we are today navigating the changing world of technology with our teens.

The World Has Changed

People have always had an issue with money. People don't naturally have the discipline to know how to handle it, and the use of credit cards and debit cards has made it harder. Money just doesn't seem as finite when it is not in your hands but in an account somewhere that you access by swiping a card.

In the generations before, if you didn't have the money to buy something, you either saved up for it or went without. No one could get themselves into too much trouble with credit. People could not spend more than they made. Everyone knew the importance of saving for a rainy day, and many practiced delayed gratification.

The easy availability of credit cards, even to college students, combined with online shopping, has made things even more difficult for young people today. When we were kids we had to load up in the car and drive to a store to look for the item. Once in the store, there was a possibility you might not find the item. I don't ever remember my parents using credit cards for everyday purchases.

Nowadays, a person can just pull up a website and have something purchased in a minute and delivered to their home in two days. How crazy is that? Today's children have to deal with constant ads 24/7 on the TV, phone, computer, billboards, etc.

Digital marketing experts estimate that most Americans are exposed to around 4,000 to 10,000 ads each day. That's equal to about four to ten every waking minute![1] The constant marketing has totally shifted the way we live. Our lives now revolve around consumption. With the increase of people using social media and smartphones, marketers are becoming even better and are now placing ads in our Facebook feed for items that we recently searched for or discussed. It's almost like they can read our minds! Advertisers have become so skilled at making us feel that our lives will be simple and complete if we just buy whatever they are selling today.

You Are the Chosen One

When my oldest started getting credit card offers a few years ago, I took a look at some of the letters. The credit card companies have a way of marketing that makes the target market feel so important. "You're selected for this offer," makes them feel like they are special. "You're on your way," makes them feel like they are going places. Plus signing up is easy. In the past a person had to mail in the application, but now you can apply online by just typing in your exclusive code and be approved for thousands of dollars of credit in under a minute.

Really take a close look at the next credit card commercial you see. How does it make you feel? The advertisers are masters at giving you the warm fuzzies and making you feel like credit is a wonderful privilege. They make us feel that if we choose their card, we are going to be able to do all kinds of fun activities and be more in control of our lives. That's not the way life works. We may be able to have almost anything we want, but we cannot have everything we want. There are trade-offs. If I choose to buy a certain item today, that means, by default, I am denying myself from something else in the future. Credit muddies the line where my spending should stop. I may feel like I have more spending power, until I realize that the credit card bills are consuming my future earnings.

Don't get me wrong, I am not an anti-credit card person. I do have one that I use, but I treat it with extreme caution. I realize that credit cards can be dangerous. If I ever had trouble paying it off every month, then I would stop using the card.

The point I am trying to make is that credit cards can be a slippery slope for young adults. So many teens leave home with very little financial training. The ones that do often have head knowledge of how to handle money but no practical experience. It's kind of like people telling you about parenting before you've experienced it. Remember before you had kids, when you would see someone's child doing something and you'd say to yourself, "My kid would never act like that!" And then you had kids. Theory is way different than actual experience. Once you are in the trenches, it's an entirely different ballgame.

Well, money is the same way. Parents can tell their kids over and over how they should save and that debt is bad, but if the child doesn't actually have to experience delayed gratification or saving for a long-term goal, what will happen when they get out on their own? Fresh out of high school or college, they are already experiencing change in so many areas. They might be living on their own, maybe learning how to cook and clean and manage their time. In the middle of processing all of these changes, we are expecting them to remember all the theoretical lessons about finances and show restraint when the credit card companies offer them a $200 cash reward bonus for opening an account and charging $500 on the card. No wonder they are struggling.

The Most Expensive Free Stuff Ever

Back when we were in college, credit card companies would be camped out all over the campus. They would be trying to get students to fill out applications in exchange for T-shirts, pizzas, frisbees, or other freebies. College students love "free" stuff. Many college students would gladly sign up for these offerings, and then find themselves hundreds or thousands of dollars in debt within a short time.

The government noticed this was a problem and created the Credit Card Accountability, Responsibility, and Disclosure (CARD) Act of 2009. This made it more difficult (but not impossible) for card issuers to market to college students on college campuses. However, they can still offer freebies if they are more than one thousand feet from the campus. The companies can go places where college students hang out and can still mail offers to them. Students are even allowed to use their student loans as income to qualify for credit cards if they don't have jobs![2] Of course, almost every major store also has a card, and some greatly encourage their shoppers to sign up. While credit card issuers may seem not to be as predatory, you still need to educate your teen so he or she is aware of credit card companies' tactics.

One of the Most Important yet Barely Taught Skills

This is serious business because your teen can manage to get themselves into thousands of dollars of debt in a relatively short period of time with little or nothing to show for it and years of work to pay it off. In my opinion, this is one of the most important life skills we can teach our teens, yet not many parents or schools are doing it. Your children are going to have to handle finances their entire lives. It doesn't matter what their career is, where they live, or whether they get married or have kids (unless they decide to become a monk or live as a hermit). Let's make sure they are equipped and prepared. We would never send them off into a battle with no weapons or training. There are money minefields everywhere that they need to be prepared to handle.

In their 2019 Money Matters on Campus Report, EVERFI surveyed over thirty thousand college students from more than 440 campuses in forty-five states, a very comprehensive sample group. In the survey, the students revealed that only 53 percent of them felt prepared to manage their money. Only 35 percent of them had ever taken a personal finance course. Many of them struggled to answer basic financial questions. Amazingly enough, even though they didn't know basic financial information, most of them really had no plans to increase their financial well-being or knowledge. Of the ones that had taken a finance course, only 55 percent of them felt that it had prepared them to manage money.

They are as lost as a goose in a snowstorm but don't see the importance of the decisions they are making every day. College is also a time of trying to fit in, and most students would not want to admit that they don't understand money principles. They think, "Obviously something must be wrong with me, because all of my friends seem to have it together." Many are struggling or naïve, but no one talks about their difficulties. They don't realize that the majority of people are also having a hard time.

Forty-six percent of those surveyed already had at least one credit card, and a third of those already had more than $1,000 in credit card debt. Even in this age of instant access via phones, only 59 percent of them regularly check their balances, and only 38 percent use a budget. So while they may have taken a course, it doesn't appear that they learned how to put it into practice in real life. With this little amount of knowledge, they are making huge financial decisions about taking on student loans and using credit cards.[3]

Another survey done by Ally Bank reinforces those numbers. This survey found that 53 percent of eighteen to twenty-four-year-olds rate their knowledge of personal finance as a C or lower. Remember, these are the kids that are moving out on their own and being targeted by credit card companies. The survey respondents said that they were twice as likely to ask friends and family for financial advice rather than use an online resource. Are they getting wise advice since there's a good chance no one has taught their friends either?

More than half of these young people also said that they would like to learn how to manage their finances better. Ally also interviewed people who were ten years past their college graduation and asked them what advice they would like to give to their college selves. The top answers were avoid student loans, learn how to understand credit cards, set and stick to a budget, pay extra on debts, and save early to take advantage of compound interest.[4]

At the Starting Line and Already Behind

According to Sallie Mae's 2019 Majoring in Money Report, the average credit card debt for college students is $1,183, and the average college graduate finishes school with $2,351 in credit card debt.[5] This does not even include the whopping $29,900 for the average student loan debt for a bachelor's degree recipient (Class of 2019).[6] They haven't even started their careers, and they are already behind.

I understand that many young people don't know about money. Maybe they just haven't learned yet, but their parents should have figured it out by now. Right? Not so much. According to a survey done by Mint, 65 percent of Americans have no idea how much they spent last month. And a third of those surveyed wished they had spent less. This lack of budgeting leads Americans to overspend an average of $7,500 a year.[7]

It's easy to convince ourselves everything is fine. We look around, and it seems like everyone else is in the same boat. With the use of credit and so much of our financial lives just numbers on a screen, we often don't see the true picture. Many of us are barely getting by, and we often fall into the trap of kicking the can down the road. Are we willing to just keep going the same way we are currently headed, hoping it all turns out in the end? That is how many people do it. Let's see how that is working for them.

According to the Experian 2020 Consumer Credit Review, the average American is $5,315 in credit card debt.[8] That may not seem so bad but realize that number does not include car or student loans. According to Bankrate, only 39 percent of Americans can come up with $1,000 to cover the cost of an unexpected emergency.[9] The importance of an emergency fund has been told to us over and over, and I'm sure you've seen it play out in real life at some point as so many people struggle with income shortfalls because of unforeseen circumstances.

Then Comes Love . . .

Let's project a little more into the future. How will this affect your teen's marriage and family? Ramsey Solutions conducted a survey in 2017 to better understand people's attitudes and behaviors regarding money. They discovered that people are bringing more and more debt into marriage. Eighty-six percent of couples married less than five years began their marriages in debt.

The number one issue couples fight about is money, and it is the second leading cause of divorce.[10] The Harris Poll also conducted a survey in 2018 of 1,400 Americans ages eighteen and older who were married or in a serious relationship. The survey found that money (36 percent) caused the most stress on their relationships.[11] I know that when we were going through extreme money problems it definitely put a strain on our relationship. Not feeling like you are making enough to provide for your family can turn a person into an angry, frustrated human. The struggle of having a tight budget and then having to pay off all your credit card debt at the same time is not a fun situation in which to find yourself. Giving our teens a strong foundation with money will definitely help them when they start a family of their own.

When the money struggles lead to divorce, the money problems get worse, not better. The average divorce costs $12,900, but it may be much higher if one of the partners contests. Also, many people don't think about all the additional costs, like the need for one person to find and furnish a new place to live, getting new cell phone service, refinancing joint loans, and therapy. Usually the standard of living drops for one, if not both parties. Plus, there are all the emotional costs the family will have to deal with for years.[12] I want to do all I can to make sure our teens avoid all those relationship struggles brought on by money mismanagement.

Two Roads Diverged

Let's look at an example of something that often happens on a college campus. Jacob, a college student, decides that he needs a new computer for school. He has no money saved so he puts it on a credit card with 16 percent interest. This is a pretty common rate. (One of the offers that came to my son had an annual rate of 25.24 percent!) Before Jacob got the card, he would have just gone without or gotten creative if he wanted to buy something. Now he occasionally uses the card on impulse buys. He is not a big spender, though, and feels like he is being frugal. He graduates college with the average credit card debt of $2,351.

If we plug those numbers into Bankrate's minimum payment credit card interest calculator, we can see how long it will take and how much it will cost to just pay off the current balance without any additional charges. His beginning monthly payment would be $94.04. It would take him eight years and two months to pay off that balance, and he would pay more than $1,000 in interest.[13] He would probably still be paying off that computer long after the computer quit working.

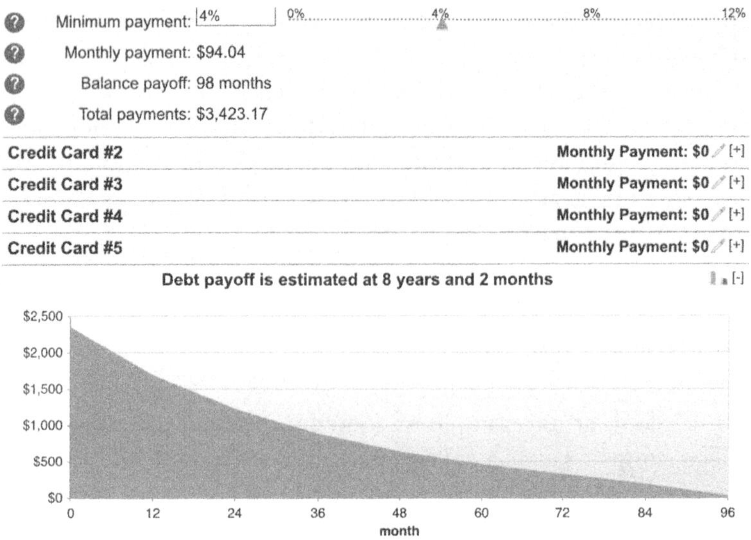

Figure 2.1. Credit card minimum payment calculator.

Now let's look at a different scenario. Jacob had a roommate in college named Ethan. Ethan's parents took a different approach. They taught him the importance of investing and starting early. He realized that the best time to start investing would be when he was young before he had a family and a bunch of responsibilities. He got into the habit of investing from the time he was fifteen and got his first job. He was working fifteen to twenty hours a week during the school year and more in the summer. He decided to put $100 into a retirement account every month. Even though he got raises and was making a lot more money as an adult, he never increased his contribution to more than $100. When he turns sixty-five, he will have invested $60,000, but his account will be worth $1,396,690.[14]

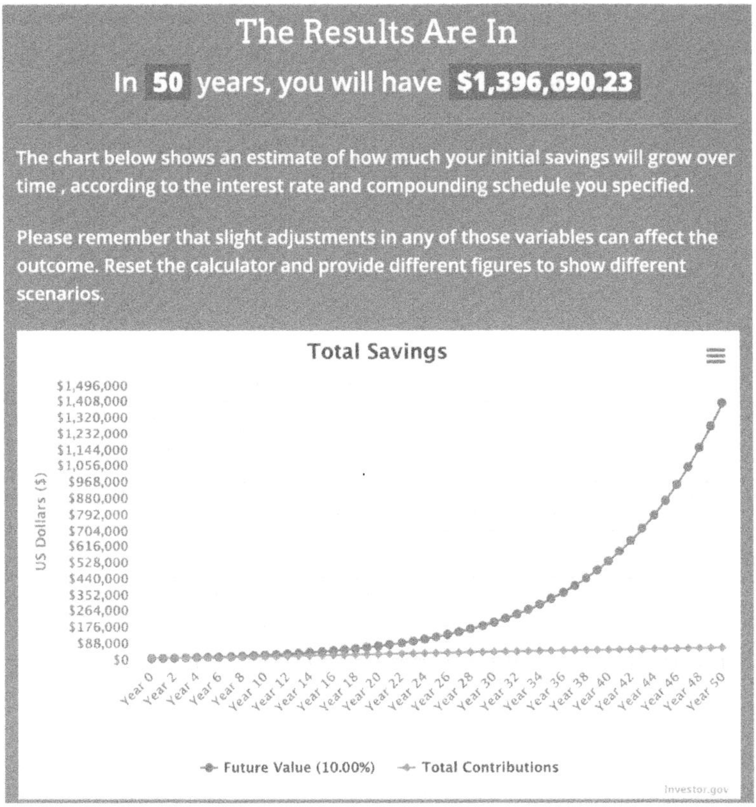

Figure 2.2. Compound interest calculator.

This is calculated at 10 percent, which is the average rate of return. This is not even accounting for a company match. We know that he is probably going to make even more money as an adult. What if he just kept investing 10 percent of whatever he made? We are talking multi-millions of dollars.

Do you see the power of compounding interest? It can either work against you (the credit card) or for you (investing in yourself). We see stories every so often in the news about people who worked low-income jobs and then died leaving behind millions of dollars to charity. Consistent investing is how they did it. Many people would say that they don't have enough money to invest. However, $100 is the equivalent of many people's cable bill or Starbucks every day on the way to work.

Think of what a difference this outlook can make in our teen's life if they harness the power of compound interest to work in their favor! I don't know about you, but I don't want my teen to be like Jacob, struggling to pay his bills and handling his money. I want him to be like Ethan, understanding the power of money early and using it as a tool to change his life, so he is not a slave to his creditors.

Reflection Questions

1. When did I get my first credit card? Did anyone really teach me about how a credit card works?

2. Could I handle a $1,000 emergency?

3. If I continue teaching my teen the way I currently am, will he be like Jacob or like Ethan?

Chapter Three
A Hidden Secret

One important key to success is self-confidence.
An important key to self-confidence is preparation.
—Arthur Ashe

Now you have seen our struggles with money and faced your own shortcomings with handling money. At this point, you may be feeling like you don't have the skills to effectively teach your children so they don't repeat your mistakes. It is a common problem, but one that can be overcome with a little bit of education and experience. I encourage you to take this as an opportunity to grow with your child.

We encountered this when our kids were younger and we had the crazy idea to build a log home as a family project. We had no construction experience other than a two-day class that we flew across the country to attend. Then we returned home to figure it out on our own. We came to realize that you can learn a lot of things on the internet and YouTube. It was a really challenging time for us because we couldn't quit. No one buys half-built log homes. There were many days we wanted to walk away when faced with an unexpected challenge. However, the experience taught us valuable lessons about ourselves and revealed that we could do more than we thought possible. The kids were learning skills along with us. I didn't think much of it at the time, but later people would comment about how our kids were different.

Several years later, we began working with kids in the foster care system. I noticed how those sweet kids often had no skills and saw how it affected them as adults. Sadly, the future would find many of them incarcerated or homeless. Then I looked around and came to the conclusion that it wasn't only foster children that were struggling. The blessings of our first-world lives have brought about some unwanted consequences. I realized that there was something important and necessary about teaching kids skills to help them succeed. We started sharing videos and began the Raising Confident Teens podcast to help teach teens and their parents life skills.

The Confidence/Competence Loop

About a year after we started Raising Confident Teens, I was listening to a podcast by author and speaker Brendon Burchard. He was talking about this very thing - learning skills leads to confidence. This is an actual psychological concept called the confidence/competence loop.[1] As soon as I heard this idea, I became excited. I had never heard anyone talk about this connection before, and just knowing about the concept has helped me become a better learner.

I wanted to share this concept because it will help as you teach your teen about money. It will also help in your life by providing a better understanding of how your own learning takes place.

In regard to the confidence/competence loop, let me start out by explaining what competence is. Brendon calls competence knowing what to do and how to do it. Have you ever met someone, and that person just exudes confidence? They probably aren't the most athletic or the best-looking, but somehow you know they are sure of themselves and their abilities. Even when faced with an unfamiliar situation, they don't seem afraid. On the other hand, you also probably know people who act in the exact opposite manner. They don't want to try anything new or are afraid of embarrassing themselves.

We often don't feel confident in our abilities, and this is how the confidence/competence loop can help. Think about the different areas of your life - job, skills, hobbies, sports, relationships. When you begin learning a skill - whether it be learning to walk as a baby, riding a bike as a child, or driving a car as a teen, you start out not knowing anything. You are nervous and have to think through every step, but eventually you can do them all without thinking.

Remember how nervous you were when you first started driving? Are you like that now? Do you even have to think about how to stop the car or turn on the windshield wipers or the headlights anymore? Remember your first job, how unsure and timid you felt? But after some time, you didn't even have to think about what to do. Your skills improved, and then you could train other people at the job. You built competence, which gave you confidence.

Researchers have found that the more confidence a person has, the more likely it is that she will be able to learn new things. If she isn't confident, she will be afraid of learning. So for every skill learned, confidence grows, which helps a person learn more skills. This doesn't apply to just one area. As a person gains competence in one area, he will become more confident in all areas.

So what about the person we talked about earlier who is not confident and is afraid of trying new things? Can this person change and become more confident? Yes. The first step in gaining more confidence is to gather knowledge by reading information or watching experts on the topic. The first step in improving your financial confidence might be to read a book on personal finance or listen to a podcast on the topic.

But we can't just stop there. Many people seemingly make a career out of learning, but never start anything. This would be like studying for your driver's permit for endless hours. You may have the driver's handbook memorized, but if you've never gotten behind the wheel, do you really know how to drive?

Take Consistent Action

The next important step is to take action. You have to know what to do and then do it consistently. Action lets you put that knowledge into practice. When we are afraid of the unknown, failure, or what others might think, we don't take action. Gathering information will help alleviate some of that fear, but the most important step is to take action. Start implementing some of the ideas and principles that you learned. Maybe that means setting up a few automatic payments or an investment account. Just getting out there and beginning will help you overcome fear. Even though failure is possible, don't give up. You are still gaining knowledge that leads to progress.

This is why I am always telling my kids that it's okay to have a bad beginning. I think people expect too much of themselves when they first start learning. That's undue pressure. Be aware of what is going on in your head. Allow both yourself and others to go through the learning phase. Tell yourself, "I can do this. I don't know how to do it yet. I'm just learning, so I'll give myself some grace, and the more I do it, the better I will become." Every time you do the action, your confidence will increase. Don't feel like you need to have everything figured out before you can even start. If you possess that mindset, you will rarely start anything.

Sir Winston Churchill, the man known for his leadership of the United Kingdom during the darkest days of World War II, once said, "Continuous effort - not strength or intelligence - is the key to unlocking our potential." The people who succeed to the highest degree are not necessarily the best or the brightest. What sets them apart is they just keep on trying.

Neuro What?

Another interesting discovery scientists have made in recent years is that our brains have neuroplasticity, a fancy way of saying our brains can change and grow. This means everyone has the potential to get better in any area, barring extreme physical or mental difficulties.

In her book *Mindset*, Carol Dweck discusses how we are born with two different mindsets - a fixed mindset and a growth mindset.[2] A fixed mindset believes that our intelligence, skills, and talents are fixed traits present at birth and can't be changed. A growth mindset assumes we can improve ourselves through effort and learning. Babies tend to possess a growth mindset. They don't care what they sound or look like; they just want to learn the skill. But as babies get older, their mindset becomes more fixed as they began to worry about what other people think.

Dweck discovered that when people with fixed mindsets experience failures or setbacks, they struggle because they feel like the situation is unchangeable. However when someone with a growth mindset faces a setback, they see the challenge as a learning opportunity. They realize that their brain is a muscle they can strengthen and grow.

Consequently, people with a growth mindset will try harder to learn and grow. I sometimes catch myself operating in a fixed mindset. For me, it is normally technology related. I find myself saying, "I'm just not good at tech." When I say that, my brain starts to reinforce what I am saying. Now I try to say, "I'm not good at tech yet, but I am learning."

Your Thoughts Have Power

This also goes along with the power of our thoughts. I used to think visualization and affirmations were kind of woo-woo. The longer I've lived, the more I've seen how what we think does determine what we become. One person can have everything going for them - talent, background, connections, opportunities, and yet not do anything with their life. On the other hand, we see people that come from a bad family background, living in the projects, with no easy opportunities, and yet they go on to achieve amazing things.

Have you ever heard a story or watched a movie about a person or people who defied terrible odds to accomplish something great? Movies like *Stand and Deliver* or *The Pursuit of Happyness* come to mind. Those people were able to achieve because they did not allow themselves to be limited by their circumstances and what other people thought. They may not have been good at something at the beginning. But they gave themselves the freedom to make mistakes and work hard and do things imperfectly, until all of those learning experiences combined to make them a success.

We have such a strong desire to be right in everything. I see this all the time with my kids. One kid will say something, and another kid will argue with him that what he said isn't right. Neither one wants to look bad and be the "wrong" one. We often ask them, "Does it really matter if you are right and he is wrong? You don't have to always correct each other and prove your superiority. As long as you know you are right, it doesn't matter." However, I catch myself doing this too. I feel the need to correct other people. If someone is telling a story wrong, I have the urge to chime in and get the facts straight.

Our brain also doesn't like us to be wrong. It operates in conjunction with what we say and works to prove us right. It does not really know the truth but will work to prove what you say is true. If you are always telling yourself that you are bad at directions or can't learn languages, it will work to prove you right.

What do you believe about yourself and money? Do you believe that you can learn to be great with money? If you don't believe that you are capable, your brain will attempt to prove you right. Let's stop all talk about, "Our family has always struggled with money," or, "I'm no good with money."

If you are not currently where you want to be with money, admit that you need to learn and be willing to change. Brian Tracy said, "If you are not willing to learn, no one can help you. If you are determined to learn, no one can stop you." Realize that no one has just accidentally become a success with money. No one just wakes up one day and knows how to handle money, or gets a new job that changes everything. It is a process, and one that you must be willing to learn. The awesome thing is that today, there are so many ways you can learn. Books, classes, online videos, podcasts - find a reliable source of information. This book could be the first step. Continue investing in yourself and in your learning, and you will reap huge rewards.

Our current constant connection to social media can also keep us from growing because we fear looking foolish. On the surface, it seems like everyone else's life is wonderful and they have no problems. Everything comes easily to them. Their children are perfect and their finances are great. Just realize that you are running your own race and you are only seeing what they want you to see.

If there is something you want to learn or improve (managing money, learning to play an instrument, learning to paint), make a plan. Give yourself grace and realize that the little actions, if done consistently, will make you more competent. This will provide more confidence, leading to more willingness to learn and the loop just gets stronger and stronger.

Don't fear failure or making mistakes, but realize that is how your brain learns and grows. Many skills do not come easily for most people. If you are struggling, it is because your brain is learning and growing. It is not wrong to come at the challenge from a different angle or to ask someone to help you. There is no weakness in that; it is better than not even trying. If a skill comes easy to you, your brain is not growing. Realize that your attitude and effort will get you farther than talent ever will. Teaching your teen to combine a growth mindset with the confidence/competence loop will make them a learning machine.

Build a Hammer

Jeannie Burlowski, author of the book *LAUNCH: How to Get Your Kids Through College Debt-Free and Into Jobs They Love Afterward*, is an academic strategist by trade. She gives students and parents this helpful analogy: "Imagine that college consists of pounding nails into boards as fast as you can. Bam! Bam! Bam-ba-bam-bam!

You'd want your hammer to be made of heavy, tempered steel and strongest oak - not spitballs and bubblegum. You get yourself the heaviest hammer by trying hard - by giving your all - in middle school and high school." Burlowski goes on to apply this same principle to financial literacy. She says, "When you practice high quality 'save-share-budget-spend-invest' financial management as a middle schooler and high schooler, you're far more likely to be good at it as an adult."[3]

Many times parents don't expect too much out of their children when they are teenagers. We want them to have fun and enjoy life, and my kids do. However, recreation shouldn't be their primary goal. They are learning how to build their hammers. They are developing discipline, intellectual ability, money skills, etc. These formative years can be a time when you work together to help them build sturdy financial hammers. Then when they are out on their own they will already know what to do and how to do it. They will not be fumbling around trying to build a hammer after the structure is partially built. Or even more important, they won't be trying to build a structure on a faulty foundation.

While we were working on the building project and probably even for a few years after, I felt like we had made a mistake. We had spent three and a half years working thousands of hours on this house that was beautiful. When sold, the house didn't make much more than it cost us in materials. It seemed like we had wasted thousands of hours of effort. However, that project taught us many lessons: If things don't work out, go back and figure out another way. You are more capable than you believe. You have more stamina than you think. You can master skills that you never imagined possible.

Looking back, peeling logs, pounding nails, and cutting boards changed us. That time in the woods was a place of healing from the crushed self-images of our past failures and gave us an amazing belief in ourselves we never would have realized if we had just sat around thinking about our past. I'm not saying that you need to go out and build a house. You can get a similar result by picking a challenging goal and making a consistent effort to achieve it.

We had no clue what we were doing most of the time, but we gained knowledge. Most importantly of all, we acted on the knowledge and gained skills. We didn't have the luxury of just gathering knowledge and sitting on it, because Mama was living in a thirty-three-foot travel trailer with four kids. I wanted to be done, so I had a goal and some major motivation. As we gained competence, we became more confident. Our perspective of the world changed, our belief in ourselves changed. An unexpected benefit happened as our kids worked alongside us. Their beliefs about their capabilities were changing too.

Nothing builds self-esteem and
self-confidence like accomplishment.
— Thomas Carlyle

Reflection Questions

1. What skill(s) have I learned in my past that I can see have given me confidence?

2. How can I use the confidence/competence loop to learn new money skills or teach new skills to my teen?

3. Do I have something I want to do or learn, but I have hesitated in taking action? What small actions can I take to get going on my dream?

4. Do I tend to operate in a fixed mindset or growth mindset?

5. Have I spent any time or money investing in my or my teen's financial education?

Chapter Four

If You Fail to Plan . . . Well, You Know the Rest

Money is only a tool. It will take you wherever you wish, but it will not replace you as the driver.

—Ayn Rand

Many people are on a journey with money, but they have no destination and no road map. How will they know when they arrive? If you decided to go on a trip and just got in your car, how would you know if you had reached your destination? Or if you knew where you wanted to go but had no map, how frustrating and time-consuming would your trip be?

Every successful endeavor must first start with a plan. When you build a house, if you don't have a plan, you will end up with a mess. In the future, if one of your kids is engaged and talking about a wedding, you don't say, "Let's just wing it and see how it goes." No, the couple sits down and looks at their budget. They plan the venue, the food, the flowers, the pastor, the music, even the chairs.

When you go on a vacation, you probably spend hours picking out the location, hotel, activities, and restaurants. I don't know about you, but food is the most vital part of our trips. And all that planning is just for a few days out of your life - a tiny speck in the grand scheme of things. My point is, amazing things rarely happen by chance. The average college graduate will earn more than two million dollars in their lifetime. Shouldn't we guide them in thinking about a plan for what to do with the money?

If you have never thought about this before, that's okay. The important thing is that you decide today to set some goals to help your teen succeed with money. I know you love your teen like I love mine. I believe that most parents want the absolute best for their kids. So why are so many young adults launching out into life with little or no training in this area? I think there are a number of reasons.

Taboo Is Not Just a Game

Many parents today never had discussions with their own parents about money, and they parent the same way. Money was a taboo subject in their household. In my research for this book, I questioned many people about what they learned about money growing up. One of the questions I often ask is, "Did your parents teach you about money?" Rarely did I ever find someone who told me that their parents intentionally taught them about money. The majority of them said, "Not at all." One person said that she asked questions trying to figure out how it all worked and was treated as though she was snooping and was told that it was none of her business. After being told that a few times, she quit asking. As a result, she ended up with a lot of unnecessary college debt and had to figure it all out on her own as an adult.

I was talking with one of my friends the other day about how she learned about money. She said the only thing she was taught was, "Save it." No further details or direction. No how-to, why, where, nothing. If we give someone directions like that, they won't see the purpose. I believe many teens are given the same instruction. They are told to save money but are given very little direction. As a result, if they do save, the money's probably just sitting in a savings account earning very little interest (actually losing money since inflation is higher than the savings rate). What if, as a teen, someone had shown her what would happen if she took $100 a month and invested it? Such instruction would have made a tremendous impact on her financial life.

Another person that I interviewed while I was writing this book was the son of a bank president. He was never taught about money at all. When he was in college, he overdrew his bank account multiple times and had to scramble to figure out how to pay the overdrafts. Even though his dad had a wealth of knowledge on the subject, money was never discussed.

Consequently, when he got out on his own, he didn't magically become a wonderful money manager. He and his wife didn't know how to handle money. This was compounded when as a young couple, they had medical challenges with their baby. With no margin in their budget and no emergency fund, they ended up bankrupt and lost their house. Already stressed because of their medical situation, they had further financial stress piled on top. In their late thirties, they finally got a handle on money, but they had to overcome twenty years of bad decisions. Can you imagine what a difference it would have made in their marriage and family life if they had learned these skills before they even left home? If they had had twenty years of compounding working in their favor instead of against them?

It might not have been as detrimental in generations past for parents to not pass on financial advice, because it wasn't as easy to get into financial trouble. There were no credit cards, and the banks wouldn't loan money to just anybody. People saved for emergencies in their "rainy day" fund. Things are different now. Unsecured debt is easy to acquire but very hard to eliminate. As a result, the majority of adults in the United States can't cover a minor emergency despite living in one of the most prosperous nations in the world. It is heartbreaking to hear stories of financial struggle, bankruptcies, and foreclosures—stress that could have been avoided if they had only known.

The sooner a young person learns about money, the stronger their financial foundation. BECU, the largest community credit union in the United States, commissioned a survey of one thousand adults and found that only 28 percent of parents are talking with their kids about finances. Many of the respondents said that fear keeps parents from talking about the subject.[1] Certainly you don't have to give your kids all the details about how much you earn, but avoiding the topic is not helping them at all. Often the only money conversation that happens is the one where the teen asks for money, and the parent just hands them a twenty. I suspect it has a lot to do with insecurity. So many parents feel like they are not succeeding in the financial area, so who are they to give advice to anyone else?

If you feel like you haven't done very well with this topic in the past, it's OKAY. This is a judgment-free zone. Have an honest conversation with your teen. Let him know that you haven't done so well at teaching these concepts in the past. Maybe you haven't been the best role model, but you want to change because you want your teen to have a good life. You want him to be smart with money and able to take care of himself. Plus he doesn't want to be living in your basement when all of his friends have apartments of their own.

Don't Expect the Schools to Teach Them

Another reason I think teens are not getting adequate training is because the schools are pushing required material for testing standards most of the time. The extra subjects, like personal finance, are the first to be cut. This is sad because every student is going to have to handle money their entire lives. Memorizing the periodic table, on the other hand, will not be something necessary for most of them to succeed.

On a brighter note, more schools are beginning to see the value in teaching the subject, and more states are making it mandatory. Twenty-one states now require high school students to take a course that integrates personal finance content.[2] Of course, the explanation of what that means varies widely from state to state. Hopefully these courses will become more widespread, because with more exposure to money training, there is a higher probability of financial success.

Although some young people are receiving training on finance in high school, many of them still don't feel prepared to manage money, as we discussed earlier. Just because they understand it in theory doesn't mean that they understand it in reality. If it is just a theoretical problem on a math paper, how well will they internalize it? We have to find a way to move it from the abstract so the light bulb goes on and they can really understand what we are talking about. Kids can't conceptualize. If it's just an exercise on a paper, it's just a math word problem.

It's Worth Your Time

Last week I was standing outside the chain-link fence at the baseball fields watching my son practice with his team. It had been a pleasant day, but as it had gotten darker, the air had gotten a little chilly. Wishing for my jacket, I looked around at the parents around me who had thought ahead and brought jackets and chairs. (I am a baseball mom newbie.) There was excitement in the air; it was the first day of practice for the year. The kids were glad to be out playing after all these months of isolation because of COVID-19. I saw other parents camping out in their chairs, chatting pleasantly, glad to see their kids out getting to do something they loved. I started thinking about all the effort we parents put into our kids and their sports. Don't get me wrong, my kids love sports, and I love watching them play. They have played soccer, volleyball, basketball, baseball, and softball.

What if we invested just a tiny bit of that same effort into teaching them a skill that will help them their entire lives, not just for a few years in school? Many sports parents know all the tricks and tips for making the season the best experience possible. Everyone starts out with no experience and builds from there. Just like I didn't think to bring a jacket, a chair, and some sunflower seeds. I also mistakenly called a run a home run (my kids could not believe I didn't know the difference). Learning is a process, in everything from baseball to money. You will be unsure and maybe not do something right. Who cares? Just as long as you are getting yourself into the game.

As parents it is easy to let the urgent get in the way of the important. We have to run them to sports practices and games, music lessons, youth activities, and church. If we aren't intentional about what we are teaching, we get so busy we forget the important lessons - the ones that they are going to need to function in society. For most of us, sports is just a very small part of our children's lives. I think exercise is important, and I love watching my kid's games. However, sports will only be a part of their lives for a very few years; managing money will be a part of their lives until they die.

You Are Enough

Don't despair, Mom and Dad, if you feel inadequate to deal with this. You are capable. The basics of money management aren't that hard. Handling money is more about behavior than it is about knowledge. You must form good habits with money and be able to discipline yourself now for a better outcome later.

I know that you may be thinking, "Why are we talking about all of this? I just want to know how to teach my teens about money." I understand. I also know that up until now you probably haven't felt like you knew how or you didn't feel capable. These concepts that we have been discussing are important building blocks of a strong money foundation for both you and your teen. If your why isn't strong enough, you won't change your money habits. If you don't know what success looks like for you and your teen in this area, how will you know if you have achieved it?

The concepts needed to win with money are not that complicated. They just require discipline. Practicing the concepts alone will help you improve your money situation. However, if you really want to improve in a better and faster way, you need to change your mindset. Remember the story that I told you about Keith and me and our climb out of debt? We were living on a budget and making better decisions, but our mindset and belief were still lacking. Our finances could have improved much faster if we had known the mindset piece of the puzzle. I feel this is an important component that needs to be discussed. Not only are our physical habits important, but also our mental habits.

Create Good Habits

F. M. Alexander said, "People do not decide their future. They decide their habits and their habits decide their future." Our lives are made up of our habits. You can take charge and control them or let them control you. You can fine-tune your habits and accomplish goals and projects better and faster. You can think about your money goals and then design your habits around your goals.

I was listening to a podcast recently with Gary Keller, founder of Keller Williams Realty and co-author of the book *The ONE Thing*. Keller is a highly successful business leader and a master at teaching people how to use habits to revolutionize their lives. He was talking about the statement "The rich get richer and the poor get poorer." Why does that happen? Is there a reason for it? He explained that if you've learned how to make money, you just repeat the action and make more money. If you are poor, you tend to repeat what you've always done, and you continue to stay poor.[3]

If you can learn the basic rules and principles around money and harness your habits to make those principles work for you, you can succeed. You are not doomed to a life of lack and frustration. If you can get your teen to see the power and the value of this from a young age - just think of all they can achieve!

Making small changes and tweaks to your life will yield dramatically better results years later. Massive success does not require massive action. It just requires consistent action over a long period of time, and the sooner we can incorporate the good habits into our lives, the better our futures will become.

If you have been fearful or worried about your own money situation, that's okay. From what we discussed so far, you can see that many people are in the same boat. The first step is to acknowledge that you want to change your life and the life of your family. Be willing to take a good look at your current financial situation. The fear of the unknown is usually much worse than the actual reality. Just take a step, action will conquer fear.

Our decisions aren't just isolated choices. Our decisions point our lives in the direction we are about to head. Show me a decision and I'll show you a direction. We've got to get good at chasing down our decisions. See where they will take us. And make sure that's really where we want to go.

—Lysa TerKeurst

Reflection Questions

1. Do I avoid talking to my kids about money? Why?

2. Am I afraid to teach my teen about money because I myself feel like I don't know what I am doing?

3. What does success with money look like for my teen? Describe how you want their future to look.

4. If I don't want them to live in my house forever, what is the plan and do they know it?

5. Am I happy with my current direction?

6. What obstacles are standing in the way of my teaching my teen?

Action Steps

1. Write out your goals. (15 minutes)

Chapter Five
The Money Plan

What you hear, you forget; what you see,
you remember; what you do, you understand.
—T. Harv. Eker

The reason you bought the book was to get the plan. You have been waiting patiently for how-tos, worried that this may be another attempt that you may fail. I just want to encourage you: you can do this, and this method doesn't have to cost any more than you are already spending. It will, however, require a little bit of effort on your part. This is not a book that you can just read through in one afternoon and then your life will be changed. It's more of a reference book that you will come back to as you refine how you teach your teen.

T. Harv. Eker's quote above really embodies the heart of this plan. We can tell teens how to handle money or even show them, but the way to get them to really internalize and understand is to get them participating. They need to take their head knowledge and put it into practice in a safe environment, like we talked about in the last chapter - putting those skills into action to build confidence.

Many parents give their children jobs or chores to teach them about money. Often the guidelines used are, "Give 10 percent, save 10 percent, and then the child can spend the rest on whatever he or she wants." This is a great first step. We also used that method with our children when they were younger, but then we took it a little further. After seeing how doing this helped our teens, we realized what an amazing teaching experience this plan provided. We want your teens to learn how to manage money, not just for their wants but also their needs.

Like we discussed earlier, people have had a hard time taking something from theory to real life without practical experience. If it's just words on the page, what makes it any different from a math word problem? Think about all the memorable learning events in your own life. You learned the most from the hands-on encounters rather than a problem you read about in a book.

Twenty years ago when we were digging ourselves out of our financial mess, I would go to the library and check out every book on personal finances available. I would devour them. At the time we only had one preschooler. I wasn't concerned about teaching him as much as I was about digging ourselves out of our financial mess. I had lots of spare time because we were living across the country from all our friends and family. We lived pretty boring lives, so I was reading all the money books I could find.

I happened to come across a book by Mary Hunt called *Debt-Proof Your Kids*, which has since been revised, and the name changed to *Raising Financially Confident Kids*. The ideas in that book made such an impact on me that when my children became teenagers, her methods of teaching her boys popped back into my head. My book is based on her concepts and takes them a little further, providing more detail for those people who struggle with taking a concept and putting it into practice.

Skills + Action = Confidence

The power of this plan is in the action. I don't learn as well when someone just tells me a concept. In fact, I will probably forget whatever I was told. Maybe that's where the phrase, "In one ear and out the other," originates. I am always telling my kids if they need something from me that they need to write it down or text me. If I'm trying to learn a new skill, I do best when I hear or read how to do it, watch someone else do it, and then do it myself.

How can we relate this to financial training? Often parents default to just lecturing their teens about money, if they talk to them at all. Apparently to a teen that often sounds like Charlie Brown's teacher. All they hear is, "Wah wah woh wah wah." It's because they don't see the connection between the lecture and real life. We want to do it differently. Let's start having conversations about money with them, as we show them how it would work practically, and then let them practice the skill on their own.

In their 2017 Parents, Kids and Money Survey, T. Rowe Price surveyed over a thousand parents across the United States and found positive money behaviors and expectations among the children were associated with their parents letting them decide how to save and spend their money on their own. The young people who managed their own money were better at delaying gratification, were more truthful to their parents about how they spent their money, didn't expect their parents to buy them their wants, and felt less shame if they didn't have things other kids owned. More than 75 percent of those kids also had regular money conversations with their parents.[1]

If you have never talked to your teen about money before and your parents never discussed money with you, the thought of these conversations may make you nervous. You may feel like you have no business trying to teach anyone about finances. Really, it is going to be fine. I am going to break it down into easy steps. Remember what we just learned. New concepts seem difficult when you first learn them. After gaining some experience, it will become easier.

The Fundamentals

Here's how the plan works. When your little darling reaches about fifth or sixth grade, you are going to actually turn parts of the budget over to them to manage. You aren't too late if your kids are older. This plan will work even with older teens as long as you are still paying for their needs. Don't freak out! We are going to learn a little at a time, and you are going to be their coach through the process. We aren't going to just lecture or expect our kids to pick up what they should do by osmosis. We are going to actually have them involved in the process so they can have years of practice under our roof with us coaching them through it.

Every parent spends money on their children. It might be for clothes, food at restaurants, youth activities, or many other things. Piper Sandler has spent the last twenty years researching teens in the United States. In their 2020 Taking Stock with Teens Report, they surveyed 9,800 teens in forty-eight states with an average age of 15.8 years. The teens reported spending $2,150 annually. The top three categories where males spent their money were food, video games, and clothing. The top three female categories were clothing, food, and personal care.[2] As these statistics show, teens are already spending money or having money spent on them. We are just restructuring the way that it is done, so it becomes a learning experience.

Let me give you an example. If your family goes out to eat once a week, and the parents normally pay, then you could calculate the average monthly cost per teen. Instead of mom and dad handling the money for their meals, now, at the first of the month the teen would receive that money to manage. When the family goes out, the teens can decide for themselves if they want to pay extra for a soft drink or buy a more expensive meal. However they may also find themselves eating off of the dollar menu at the end of the month if they didn't manage their money well.

Your first assignment is to figure out what you are currently spending on your teen. Many families spend in these categories:

Spending money	School supplies
Treats/Snacks	Toiletries
Birthday gifts	Makeup
Church or youth activities	Haircuts
Christmas gifts	Gasoline
School lunches	Senior Trip
Concessions	Meals out
Clothes/Shoes	Cell phone

You can also find this checklist in the appendix and online at https://rachelmurphycoaching.com/book-resource. Check the categories in which you are currently spending money on your teen. Don't get overwhelmed. I put a lot of categories on the list. You probably won't be using all the categories; I don't. You also won't be using very many of these if your teen is younger or just starting out. Remember, the goal is to help them become independent gradually and in a safe place where their mistakes won't be so painful.

In this book we are going to use two young people to illustrate the steps as we go through them. They are both just starting the plan. The first one is Matthew, who is a twelve-year-old sixth grader, and Emily, who is a sixteen-year-old tenth grader.

Here is Matthew's category list:

Spending money
Treats/Snacks
Birthday gifts
Church or youth activities
Christmas
Meals out
Concessions
Clothes/shoes
Toiletries
Music lessons

Matthew is homeschooled, so his family doesn't have to worry about school supplies or school lunches. His mom cuts his hair, and he is too young to worry about the prom, a cell phone, or gasoline.

Here is Emily's category list:

School supplies
Homecoming/prom
Birthday
Church or youth activities
Christmas gifts
Gasoline
Car insurance
Clothes/shoes
Makeup/Toiletries
Cell phone
Music lessons
Haircuts

Emily has some pretty severe food allergies, so the family rarely buys outside snacks or food out. They also don't give their kids spending money. Their kids work extra jobs for fun money.

Your next assignment is to take your listed categories and look at our recommended categories by grade. These worksheets are available in the appendix or online at https://rachelmurphycoaching.com/book-resource. This will give you an idea of where to start. I added Charity and Savings to these lists in case you want to make those a part of your plan. Of course if you add those categories it will bump your teen's monthly salary higher.

Next, take the blank categories worksheet (also in the appendix) and write down the categories you are going to use, and then, as well as you can, figure out what you actually spend. Only begin with one or two categories to ease into the plan. You might want to look at receipts or bank or credit card statements to jog your memory. Most important, don't stress out - the numbers don't have to be exact. Try to keep it close to what you are currently spending though. Now is not the time to decide to cut expenses. You don't want your teen resenting the plan because all of a sudden you have reduced the amount of money they get for clothes or spending money.

Don't feel like you have to do all the categories. In fact, you shouldn't start out with too many. Doing so will just overwhelm you and your teen. If you are starting out with older teens, give them a few categories. If they handle that well, add a few more in a month or two. The goal is progress, not checking off the list that they have a certain number of categories turned over to them. If you got a late start and your teen is about to graduate and you are only doing half the categories, your teen will still be more prepared than most young adults.

Matthew's parents decided to start with Charity, Savings, Spending Money, and Treats/Snacks. They had been giving him a little spending money every week, and once a month the family would go out for ice cream. They also would go to the gas station three or four times a month for Icees. Here is his worksheet:

Charity	$4
Savings	$4
Spending Money	$20
Treats/Snacks	$12
Total	$40

Note: we encourage our teens to save 10 percent and give 10 percent to a worthy cause. Some of you may get tripped up on the charity/savings categories and figuring out 10 percent. If money isn't tight, you can just round up to a higher total salary if you want them to give or save a certain percentage of their income. If money is tight or you have trouble figuring those amounts out, you can just start out without those two categories and add them in later when you are more comfortable. Or another alternative is to use a flat amount instead of a percentage.

Emily is older and will be able to handle more categories, but to begin with, it is best just to do a few to get started. Her church youth group gets together for an activity once a month, so her parents felt that would be a good starting category. She is also always wanting to buy makeup and her own special soaps and lotions, though she probably already has enough to start her own Bath & Body Works. Her parents decide to turn that over to her discretion along with her other toiletries, like toothpaste, deodorant, and hair products. Since she is older, they will reevaluate in three to six months and probably add in a few more categories if she is doing well. Here is her worksheet:

Charity	$6
Savings	$6
Youth activities	$23
Makeup/Toiletries	$25
Total	$60

At our house we increase our teen's salaries and categories at the start of the school year, but you could do it based on their birthday or at the beginning of the year. Do what works for you.

As your teen gets older, they will have to learn to account for more expenses that may not occur every month but still have to be in the budget. An example of this kind of expense would be auto insurance.

Many insurance policies are paid twice a year. If you don't figure this expense into your monthly budget, it will surprise you. You have to learn to set some money aside and not touch the balance because it may be needed later.

There are a number of categories where the money doesn't get spent every month, such as clothing, haircuts, Christmas, gifts, and car savings/repairs. These are the categories that seem to cause the most trouble for people in their budgets. It is important to learn how to manage those variable expenses. If it is an ongoing expense, you may have to estimate the expense until you accumulate a record of past spending. Try to figure out how much you spent for the year and then divide by twelve to determine how much you should set aside to save each month. If it is a one-time expense, you need to calculate how much you think the total cost will be and divide by the number of months that you have to save to determine how much you need to set aside every month.

This makes occasions like Christmas way more enjoyable because the event is paid for over time. You may end up with a pile of money in your account, but you have to remember that it is all designated for the future. It may be helpful to set up a sub-account if possible so you don't feel like you have all of this money available for a big shopping spree. Most budgeting apps allow you to divide your income into categories and have the ability to automatically roll the leftover from the current month into the next month's category.

To help you get a better idea of what you spend on your teens and to prepare for future categories, you can use the spending tracker. Every time you spend on something related to your teen, record the date, what it was for, and the amount.

Starting the plan is the hardest part. There is a learning curve. The first couple of months will be a little challenging because you are doing something new. Remember, you are building competency in this process too. Once you are several months into the plan, the process will be mostly automatic.

Let Them See That You Trust Them

More likely than not, you are going to have a teen that blows money when he first starts. Your response to this is important. Be strong! Do not bail your teen out. If he spent all his lunch money on a video game, then he is going to have to pack a lunch. For this reason, we don't begin with categories that will cause a big problem if the teen blows it. Maybe you normally give your teen money whenever they want to run to the store for snacks. Now you just give your teen all the money for the month once, at the beginning of the month. If he blows it right away, the only one he hurts is himself.

This is a great way to show your teens that you trust them. You may be terrified on the inside, but you can't let them know that. They may have never experienced freedom with no restraints. Expect them to go a little crazy. Your child is going to make mistakes (no probably about it). When that happens, don't lecture or bail them out. As much as you want to say something, restrain yourself. When you mess up, you don't want a lecture. Words like, "I told you not to spend all your money on junk," or, "You are so careless," are not helpful. Say them inside your head to yourself, if you must. The best response is something along the lines of, "Aww, you spent all your money for the month on junk food for your friends. That's too bad. I'm sure you'll figure out a way to earn more money," and walk away. They are learning the lessons. Think about your own life. The best lessons came from mistakes and consequences. If you bail them out, they won't suffer the pain of their decisions. And if they don't learn while they are safe at home in high school, will college or career be a better environment to learn the lessons?

Even if you have a teen that is very responsible, they will occasionally mess up or not use their brain. Research says that the prefrontal cortex of the brain, which is responsible for decision-making, is not fully developed until the age of twenty-five. Even with kids that have it all together, expect them to occasionally do things that don't make sense. When I was in college, I belonged to a Christian campus organization. During the summer many of us would go all over the world and do missions work - summer camps, Vacation Bible Schools, etc.

My best friend in college and I somehow both ended up on a team together in the Black Hills of South Dakota. When we were at the airport waiting to leave, my friend's mom was giving her a lecture about being responsible and how she needed to stick with me because I was the responsible one. All of a sudden, in a panic, I looked her mom straight in the eyes and said, "I forgot my ticket." Her mom just rolled her eyes and shook her head and, I'm sure, prayed we would make it back alive. I usually was dependable, but we all have our moments. Expect them. That way you won't be caught off guard when they happen. When my kids have a moment, I just mutter to myself, "Prefrontal cortex," and I feel better.

P.S. Don't announce today to your kids, "I just read a book with some great ideas, and here is how we are going to do it." Wait until you finish the book. In the next chapter we are going to discuss some guidelines that you might want to consider. Have your plan before you present it. I'm not saying that you have to have a perfect plan, because if that is your goal, you will never achieve it. But think through the steps and go in with a plan. Also, if you are married or have an ex who shares custody, you need to be on the same page.

Action Steps

1. Fill out the current spending checklist. (5 minutes)

2. Pick a few (and only a few) categories from your list to start. You can reference the recommended categories by grade list to get an idea of where to start. (5 minutes)

3. Write the categories you have chosen on the blank categories worksheet, or print one out from our website. Decide how much you are currently spending in those categories and write it on the worksheet. (20 minutes)

4. Start filling out the Spending Tracker. (ongoing)

Chapter Six
Because All Teens Look for Loopholes

You don't rise to the level of your goals,
you fall to the level of your systems.
—James Clear

Guidelines

We all know how teens like to get us on technicalities. For that reason, it's best to think through your guidelines beforehand so there is no confusion later. We didn't do this with our oldest when we started the plan. If we had done so, transitions would have been easier for both us and him. Let them know the rules. They need to be clear about what you are paying for and what categories are their responsibility.

Here are some questions to help you come up with your guidelines.

- **At what age will you start? When will it end? Will you stop after high school? College?**

This is a personal family decision. It depends on the maturity of your child. Some kids who are very responsible and mature could start earlier. Other kids may need a few more years until they are ready. The same thing goes for the end date. There is really no right or wrong as long as there is a communicated expectation of the end date. They need to know it is coming and have time to prepare for their next steps.

- **Will job employment change their salary?**

Once they start working, will they be responsible for paying for some of their categories that have been previously funded by you? Or will you keep their salary the same and let them use that money to fund other things such as college or a car?

- **How much do you require them to save and give to charity?**

These were categories I wanted to include in our plan. If you include these categories as part of their salary, it will increase the amount you spend on your teen, so this is an individual decision. These concepts are important habits that I wanted to ingrain in my kids early. I never really made it an option for them; it was expected.

My teens automatically save 10 percent in long-term savings. This will go toward their purchase of a first car. They will see the effects of what a few dollars here and there saved consistently can accomplish. This also helps them get into the mindset that they don't have to spend everything they earn.

In our family we have decided that giving is just something we always do. We want it to be their giving, not just handing them some of our money to put in the offering. Giving helps them see that money is not all for spending on themselves and their wants. We allow them to use their giving for whatever they want as long as it is a real need. They sometimes give at church. However, they have also used their giving money to make care baskets for friends who were very sick and in the hospital, given to a friend's family whose parents' business was shut down by COVID, and bought gift cards for gas, groceries, and fast-food restaurants for friends' families who have major medical needs.

- **Will you help them with the purchase of a car? How much?**

Don't feel like you have to provide any help. It's not a right. For our family, we will match what our teenagers earn up to a certain amount for their first car, but the car must be bought before college ends. You don't want them to be thirty years old and coming to get you to pay for half a car. We like for our teens to pay for half of the cost of their cars because it gives them a sense of ownership. They are more interested in the car-buying process, they shop around, and they take better care of the car.

- **Will you allow debit cards? Or credit cards?**

When they first begin the plan, I would start out with paper money. Paper money is better than debit cards for visually seeing where your money is going. It is proven that people spend more when they use a card. After they get comfortable with the plan, then you can introduce a debit card. A lot of banks will allow your teen to have a debit card at the age of twelve or thirteen. Our credit union actually just started giving debit cards to eight-year-olds.

Our teens use debit cards. It makes it so much easier to keep up with where the money went and to transfer money to their accounts, but they all started with cash. I would use extreme caution when giving any teen a credit card.

- **Are you just going to do the very basics?**

You might have certain amount you are willing to spend on the necessities kids need. For example, you might tell them, "I will give you a set amount for clothes. If you want fancy shoes, you will have to pay the difference." This will depend on your family and how you do things. In our family, we don't have a bare-bones budget. However, I absolutely would do one if money was tight. This would ensure my kids were still learning how to manage money, but their clothing budget would be based on thrift store prices.

We also don't give an extravagant budget. I want them to have to work at making their budget balance. My kids get a basic budget, and if they want extra, they have to work for it. All of them have side jobs occasionally. Hudson and Jenna have an online business with their uncle, and they mow lawns. Hudson does odd jobs and repairs small engines. Rebecca sometimes bakes and sells desserts. The girls also babysit and clean houses. Rebecca also had a part-time job at a local pizza parlor.

- **Will we have any restrictions on what they can buy?**

By restrictions I mean, are you going to give them free reign with their salary to buy whatever they want? If not, then you might need to clarify this at the beginning, especially if you have one that likes to push the boundaries. At our house, you still have to abide by our rules. You may get to manage the money, but you don't get to buy inappropriate clothing or get a tattoo or anything like that.

- **Will you tie chores into any of their salary?**

I give my children a very basic salary so they can purchase all their needs that we would normally buy (clothes, haircuts, birthday gifts for friends, etc.). Since money isn't as tight as it used to be, I do give them more than I would have in the past. For example, if they are in sports, I give them the equivalent of a couple of dollars per home game for concessions and enough for a meal for each away game. If money was tighter, I wouldn't give them money for home games. One of my teens never spends her home game money; she always packs snacks. Her sister always spends hers on concessions.

I don't really give them a lot of spending money. They all help around the house, and they can earn additional funds by doing extra chores. If I started having trouble with things getting done, then we would have a talk about docking their bonus pay or taking away privileges. The salary shouldn't be taken away for bad behavior. Just like you buy your kid's clothes or get them school supplies even if they misbehave, don't take their salary away or threaten to take it away. Think through all the guidelines so that when you explain the plan to your teen, you can cover all the bases.

Money Plan Form

After you decide on your family's rules, fill out a money plan form for the year. This form is included in the appendix and online. We have various forms depending on if they are going to have a checking and savings account or just a savings account. There is a place for them to list a long-term goal they are working toward. I write suggested amounts on my teens' forms for what I think should go into each category to give them a starting point, but they ultimately decide the amount.

This form helps them know exactly what they are responsible for over the course of the year. These amounts are not set in stone. My teens will move stuff around if they know there is something they want to buy or do. For example, if all their friends are going to an event, they might choose to take some of their clothing money this month and put it toward the event. Isn't that the kind of stuff we do with our budgets as adults?

I encourage them to try save extra money for unexpected things that come up that they want to do or buy. A couple of them have a miscellaneous fund for such expenses. I also encourage them to save up an emergency fund. An emergency fund is exactly what it sounds like — a fund for unexpected emergencies. I don't give my teens money specifically for their emergency funds. It's their responsibility to figure out how to fund that category. When they make extra money, they often put a portion of the money into their emergency fund.

One of my teens ran over my cell phone with a riding lawnmower recently. We had dropped them off to mow a customer's lawn, and I had told her several times to put the phone in their lunchbox. She left it in her pocket, and the phone fell out. She was so upset about it that I felt that I needed to balance grace with responsibility. She was totally willing to pay for it, but I could see that she had learned a lesson. If I hadn't told her several times to put the phone in the lunchbox, I would have probably just paid for it myself. However, we worked out a compromise. I only had to pay $100 to replace the phone because I had just bought it and had insurance. So we split the cost, and she used her emergency fund.

The amounts you put into each category will depend on your family and your lifestyle. I would advise you to try to keep the amount you are currently spending on your teen consistent. It's the same money just funneled through a new middleman. If you normally buy them $50 worth of clothes a month, that's how much should go in the clothing category. The intent is not to save money; the intent is to teach your child how to manage money. Try to be as reasonable as you can.

Automation Is Your Friend

Learning the power of automating your financial life may help not only your teen, but also you. The more you automate your finances, the easier life will become for you. I have gotten to the point in my finances where so many things happen automatically. Thanks to current technology, you can have almost all of your bills and giving paid automatically, your paychecks auto-deposited, and your investments automatically deducted. The more you can do this, the less stress on your brain.

When you first start the plan, I suggest that you pay your kids in cash. The brain processes cash better than money spent on a debit card. After you and your teen have gotten into the rhythm of the plan, you can begin to automate their salary. Set up an automatic transfer from your account into your teen's account every month. If you set up minor accounts under your account, then you should be able to set up automatic transfers easily.

In my house, the older teens who have both a savings and checking account have 10 percent of their salary deposited into their savings and the remainder put into their checking account. The younger kids get certain categories in cash (spending, giving, food out), and the rest gets put into their savings. If they need to spend something from one of the other categories, they ask to transfer it out of their savings account. I keep some cash on hand and just transfer the money from their savings account to my account and give them the cash. You can easily keep up with how much they have in each category with an app. Or you can use old-fashioned pen and paper.

Getting your teen to see the power of automatically depositing money into savings will change their financial future. Now is the best time for them to form these habits before they have all of the responsibilities of adulthood. If they can become accustomed to only living off of 80 or 90 percent of their income and make that a practice instead of spending every penny (or more) of what they make, their lives will be radically different. It's a lot harder to start saving once you have the biggest mortgage and car payment you can afford.

One of the best tactics is to have money automatically taken out and put into a savings account or 401(k) that is harder to access. It is normal human behavior to be lazy and procrastinate, and these days distraction is a constant struggle. If you have to log into your account and transfer funds to savings/investments every month, more than likely you won't do it. Make your teen aware of that tendency and show them how they can use that in their favor. Once a system is set up that does the saving and investing automatically, it will be too much trouble to change, and you will save money with no effort.

Your teen's monthly salary needs to be reliable, just like your paycheck. It needs to come on the same day every month. As parents, it can be easy to say, "I don't have the cash on me. We'll do it next week." That is comparable to your boss telling you that he is going to pay you a week late. Paying on time is a good way to build trust. Sure, emergencies may come up, but do your best to make this a priority.

Also, I would fill out two copies of the money plan every year — one for them and one for you. They may lose theirs, and you may want to reference it later. I look at our plans pretty often because I can't remember salary and category amounts. Also, if you have multiple children, you might want to have a record of what categories and how much you paid the older sibling. It is probably a good idea to have a file somewhere with all your budgets, rules, and agreements.

Monthly Budget

Once your teen is managing several categories, it would be a good time to introduce them to creating a monthly budget. The advantage of starting as a teen is that it is relatively simple because they don't have a large income or many expenses. It won't take a great deal of time to calculate or be too stressful. Their budget will slowly grow over the years along with their income and expenses.

For many years I used a paper budget, and you could teach your teen budgeting that way. There is a paper budget in the appendix and online, in case you would like to go that route. However, most teens these days have phones, and may find an online budget easier. If they have a budgeting app on their phone, they can know exactly how much money they have available and can record their transactions immediately.

A basic teen budget is simple. They just need to input their Money Plan salary plus any additional money that they receive from a job or gifts as income. Then they can list out their required categories in the expense section. If they have extra money from work or gifts, they should decide where they want it to go ahead of time. Otherwise, it has a way of disappearing. A good method of dispersing the extra is to give themselves a percentage to just blow on fun stuff and put the rest towards a big savings goal like a car or college. The teenage years can be a great time to save money since the majority of them don't have all the expenses of an adult.

There is no perfect method of budgeting that works for everyone. The perfect budget is the one you will use. Some people like things easy. The simplest method uses three buckets – savings, bills, and everything else. Other people like to do spreadsheets and have many different categories. No one way is better than another; you may have to experiment with several different methods to find the one that works best for your teen.

Finance apps can be a great way to manage the details of a budget. Two free good apps that I recommend are Ramsey Solutions Every-Dollar and Goodbudget. Both of them are accessible through a web browser or on an Android or Apple device. Either of these free options would be a great introduction to budgeting for your teen. EveryDollar and Goodbudget also have paid programs, but I have no experience with those.

EveryDollar has the ability to have unlimited envelopes and categories. You can move your most-used categories to the top of the list, making it easier to access them. In addition, the app gives feedback showing percentages of spending for the month so you can see if you are overspending in a category. Some of the downsides of EveryDollar are that you must have an internet connection to access the app, and no report feature is available in the free version. It also only does a monthly budget and carries over the same budget amounts from the previous month.

Goodbudget has the ability to work even without internet service. Categories can be set up to refill not only monthly, but also semi-monthly, weekly, or every two weeks. The app prefills the names of the stores you spent at when you start typing them. It gives you feedback when you are doing well or tells you that you need to stop spending if you are going over budget. Plus it has a reports function so you can see how you spent your money. The drawbacks of Goodbudget are that you are limited to twenty categories/envelopes, and it is a little less intuitive than EveryDollar.

If you want to use paid software, I highly recommend You Need a Budget (YNAB). They offer a one-month free trial, so you can give it a test before purchasing. The cost is $84 a year, but each member of the family can have their own separate budget within your account. This app will link to your bank accounts, so you are less likely to miss transactions, and it makes reconciling easier. I started using it last year and have really enjoyed it.

Unlike other budgeting software, YNAB encourages you to only allocate the money that you actually have in your possession to spend. You don't forecast what you think you might have for the month or look back at the end of the month and see, "Oops, I blew the budget again." It is more proactive rather than reactive. It lets you see all of your different financial accounts in one place on the side so you know your exact totals. There are many video tutorials on how to use it, and most of them are hilarious. Anytime I can laugh while learning about money, it's a good thing. All of our teens use and love YNAB.

There is an app that has recently come out called Qube. It is like the cash envelope method but digital. This method is known for being a great way to help a person stop overspending and stay on budget. When a person uses the cash envelope system, they take actual envelopes and write a category name like groceries or dining out on each of them. Then they put the cash they have allocated for the spending period for that category in the envelope. When the cash is all gone, they have to either stop spending or reallocate money from another category. Qube has all the benefits of using the envelope system without the drawbacks such not being able to track spending and having to carry around large amounts of cash. I am testing the free version myself right now, and I have been very impressed.

To use Qube, a person opens up an account with Choice Financial Group (Qube's FDIC insured bank) and is mailed a debit card. The debit card holder direct deposits a paycheck or transfers money from another account and then places their money into categories (qubes) in the app. When they go to make a purchase, they open up a qube and the bank transfers the money to that category. After the purchase is complete, they close the qube and the money goes back to the bank. There is no money on the debit card except when the qube is open, so Qube is much safer than a regular debit card. If someone were to just find your card they wouldn't be able to spend any of the money because you have to open the qube in the app before purchase.

If you have a teen who is over eighteen, the free individual account is a good option, especially if they struggle with staying on budget and making thoughtful money decisions. Qube is planning on releasing a paid family version in the fall of 2021. It will allow up to ten teen/kid cards. This option might be something that you want to keep in mind for your family.

The great advantage to all of these budgeting apps is that they allow your teen to allocate their money into different categories in their budget. Then they can get into the habit of just checking the amount available in each category. This is easily done with the app. Many people get themselves into trouble because when they want to buy something they look at their bank account and say, "There's $1,000 in my account. Of course I can afford this shirt." This often leads to other problems when they don't have enough money for later expenses. If your teen learns from the start to give every dollar a name, they will not get trapped trying to juggle their income and expenses.

Monthly Checkup

At the end of every month/beginning of the next month is a great time to have a little checkup with your teen and discuss how it is going. I sit down for just five or ten minutes with my teens, and we reconcile their accounts. They have been on the plan for years, so they have all transitioned from getting paid in cash to having everything automatically deposited into their savings and checking accounts. They keep a little money on hand for places that are cash only, like concession stands at their games. They do track their cash account in their app. Since their debit cards are linked to YNAB, reconciling is really easy. They just hit the Reconcile button, and the program asks them, "Is your current account balance $345.67?" Then they click Yes or No. If the answer is no, they have to go on a scavenger hunt to find the missing transaction. However, the amount has never been off. They do that for their savings and their checking accounts. It's a super easy process. They don't have many transactions, making it a painless way to get them into the habit of adulting.

If you have a teen who struggles with keeping up with where they spent their money, you might want to try this tactic. Tell them, "Next month's salary will be based on this month's records. Your salary will be the amount of the transactions from the month that are recorded on your paper budget or in your app."

Agreement Form

After you have decided on your rules and budget, call a family meeting and discuss and explain the program. You could be official if you want and sign an agreement together. We have also included a sample agreement form that you can use in the appendix as well as online, if desired. If you sign an agreement, I would print out two copies, one for them and one for you. Make a big deal about it, especially if they are in the younger grades. Emphasize that this is a big step in their becoming an adult. It will help them be able to apply the money principles you want them to learn. Older teens might not want to do this; they might think it is hokey.

It is important that you don't give in if they balk at the idea and that you emphasize the importance and reason for doing this: to teach them to plan ahead of time and be intentional with their money. I think once they try it and see the independence it gives them, they will be more agreeable to participating.

Action Steps

1. Decide on your family's guidelines (with the other parent if applicable). (30 minutes)

2. Fill out a money plan. Don't overthink this form. You are just starting. They should only have a couple of categories. (20 minutes)

3. Decide on a paper budget or a budgeting app. You can ease into this over the next few months. (20 minutes)

4. Schedule and have a family meeting to introduce the program to your teen. This would be the time to sign an agreement form, if you so choose. You set the tone. Make it fun and exciting! Yummy snacks always help. (30 minutes)

Chapter Seven
Challenges and Changes

A pessimist sees the difficulty in every opportunity; an optimist sees the opportunity in every difficulty.
—Winston Churchill

As you work through this plan with your teen you will encounter some challenges and changes. Expect them, it's a part of every learning experience.

It's a Blessing and a Curse

Many years ago we used to love to watch the show Monk. If you've never seen the show before, the main character is a brilliant germaphobe detective played by Tony Shalhoub who struggles with obsessive-compulsive disorder and a slew of phobias ranging from dryer lint to sleeveless T-shirts. He has an amazing ability to notice obscure details, but those details often distract him from solving the case. When people comment on his abilities, he often says, "It's a blessing and a curse." He can unravel great mysteries, but he also has to deal with all of that information in his brain.

The money plan you design for your teen operates in a similar manner. I know many people just want someone to do all the work for them — but that is not the way the plan works. This plan is tailored to fit you and your lifestyle, whether you shop at the thrift store or Louis Vuitton. You have to figure out how much you are spending on your teen and decide on your own numbers.

If I were to give you an amount for each category, you would probably either say, "It's not enough. This won't work for me," or, "It's too much, my budget is tight. This won't work for me." The beauty is that you can customize it to fit the season of life you are in and your budget. It can also be a curse because you do have to do some of the groundwork at the beginning. I tried to make it as easy as possible for you by providing worksheets and walking you through the plan. You still have to do the work, but really, once you get in the habit it isn't that hard. I probably spend less than twenty minutes a month doing this with my three teens.

Change Your Mindset, Change Your Future

The biggest way to move the needle for your finances is to change your mindset. You can look at money as a blessing, or you can look at it as something that will hold you back. It doesn't take much to learn how to handle money. Money is neither good nor evil. It isn't even the goal. It is just a tool we use to achieve our goals. The hardest part of money management is forming good habits and discipline. Winning with money doesn't mean that you have to live a life of sacrifice and deprivation. It does mean that you need to be intentional and plan how to spend your money.

Could you unconsciously be avoiding money issues? Often I procrastinate on things that I know I should be doing. If a task feels overwhelming to me, I often find myself doing other things. It's not that I am doing something wrong, but I have come to realize these are delay tactics. For me, my method of delay is housecleaning. It feels justified because we need a clean house, right?

When I get right down to it and face what I am avoiding, I can often get the dreaded task done in far less time than I was expecting. You may do the same with facing your money challenges. Bob Hawke says, "The things which are most important don't always scream the loudest." Make sure that you don't neglect the important just because it doesn't seem urgent.

What a great opportunity to teach your teens how to start their financial lives off on the right foot being thoughtful and intentional with their money decisions! You are combining two powerful learning strategies - modeling and practical application. If you've never really taken control of your money, you will feel awkward at first. Any new skill has a learning curve until you build confidence, and you are going to make mistakes. Expect the mistakes, and don't let them derail you. Sloppy success beats perfect failure every time.

Handling money is not some kind of talent that only a few people are born with. It is a learnable skill. As someone who was once financially defeated and hopeless, I just want to say that it is worth it! I am putting out my hand and reaching back to you to tell you that you don't have to live a life that is a financial mess. It is possible to change your family and start the beginning of a new legacy. One that wins with money, no matter what circumstances you as a parent have experienced. And the most important part of the puzzle is believing that you can do it!

Perfection Is the Enemy

So many people feel so restricted by a budget. Let's change the way we think about it. It is not telling us we can't spend money; it is telling us we can spend and how much. When I didn't have a good budget, I felt guilty about everything I spent. Now if I spend money on clothes, I don't feel bad because everything else is funded. I know how much is in the clothing category, and I'm not having to rob from another category.

Maybe you don't like the word *budget*. It often carries such negative connotations. Some people use the word *spending plan*. This expresses a sense of "I am going somewhere. I know the direction I am headed. I am being intentional." Whether you use the word *budget*, *plan*, or something else, I want to talk about the idea that people feel they need to craft the most perfect plan. They spend hours and hours perfecting the plan, and then they feel bad if they ever have to change it. I am a bit of a nerd myself and receive some kind of strange satisfaction from crunching numbers too. I have often found myself falling into the trap of trying to craft a perfect budget.

Life is fluid and ever-changing, especially with kids. You must give yourself permission to be flexible. I am constantly tweaking and changing my budget. True, some expenses are the same every month, but others aren't. Our teens need to realize this so they don't feel like failures if their budget is not perfect. Also, they need to give themselves permission to move things around. As long as they are saving and funding all categories, they have permission to alter the plan. I have one teen who is very frugal and tries not to spend. She takes any extra money she can from her other categories to put into her car savings; that's okay. Altering the plan doesn't mean you failed.

The Only Mistake Is Doing Nothing

Learning flexibility will help your teen when they get older and are doing all of their own finances. Many people decide to get their finances in order and are all excited. However, a week in when things don't go perfectly, they totally ditch their plan. Then they fall back into their old ways, getting further and further into debt. We want our teens to realize that their budget is an ever-changing plan that will help them reach their goals. There is no exact right way to do this plan as long as it works for you and you are making progress.

People are afraid to do the wrong thing, so they do nothing. Making a mistake or miscalculating isn't failure. Make your best guess and readjust along the way. We can't predict the future. There have been times when I realized that I didn't give my teens enough for a certain category, so I went back and adjusted. Tip: it's better to start low and add than to start too high and take away. You will make mistakes and readjust, but it will get faster and easier the more you do it. Don't let perfection keep you from getting started.

I'll Have the Water, Please

One of my friends told me a story about her six-year-old little girl. My friend would stop at Starbucks to get a drink and would occasionally buy her little girl a cake pop. Someone had recently given her daughter some money as a gift. Shortly after, my friend and her daughter stopped at Starbucks to get my friend a coffee. The little girl asked if she could have a cake pop, and her mom said, "Why don't you use your money?" The little girl replied, "I wouldn't want to waste my money."

An amazing transformation happens when it goes from being Mom and Dad's money to my money. We have seen it in our own teens' lives. They become way more thoughtful about their purchases and less impulsive. It also eliminates so much of the stress that revolves around money.

We have five kids, and money was pretty tight when they were younger. When we went out to eat, everyone often drank water. If they had a choice, most of them would have chosen to drink something else. They usually had a good attitude about it, but I always felt like I had to defend the "we are all getting water to drink" speech. A funny thing happened as that part of the budget got turned over to them. When it became their money, I would hear them tell the waiter, "I'll have water, please." They realized that if they didn't spend the money on a drink, they could use it for something else. It also eliminated all the guilt that I felt for making everyone drink water.

Clothing is also a category that causes a lot of stress between parents and teens. Teens often want to spend more money on the more expensive brands, or maybe they are always wanting to buy the latest thing everyone is wearing. Then parents spend the time and money to buy clothes, and the teen may or may not wear them.

If you make clothing a budget item, you won't have to deal with the drama. Your teen will start to become a lot more thoughtful about clothing purchases. She won't tend to buy clothes that she isn't going to wear. If she doesn't like the clothes, she will make sure to take them back. If she wants a more expensive brand and her salary doesn't allow for such an expense, she can earn money to make up the difference. The parents aren't upset because they wasted money on unworn clothes or the latest fads, and Mom doesn't have to feel guilty for not buying the latest fad.

Something teens so desperately want is to be independent and in control. Using the money plan allows them to feel this way. I remember hating to ask my parents for money when I was a teen, even if it was for something I needed. Sometimes I would go without just because I hated asking. My teens love the plan. They don't have to come and ask me for money for every little thing. They get to decide if they want to spend it or not. If they are frugal and save, they get rewarded. Normally if a teen finds deals and doesn't spend all of Mom and Dad's money we had planned to spend, he doesn't see any benefit. He is only saving money for his parents. If, however, teens are in charge of the money, they get the reward of saving and finding deals. And what teen doesn't want to be able to just whip out their wallet and pay for something without having to ask for money and permission?

In the book *Atomic Habits*, James Clear discusses how to stop a bad habit. He explains that we are more likely to avoid an experience when the ending is painful.[1] Well, if Mom and Dad always pay for everything and my being wasteful or extravagant never hurts me in any way, then I'm not going to change.

By having their own money and having to budget it, your child will learn amazing lessons that can only be learned through experience - concepts like how to plan ahead and how to delay gratification. Not to mention the most important concept that so many people have not yet grasped - how to live on less than you make. These concepts are not things that can be learned from a book. They have to be learned by experience, and the smaller the consequences, the better for the teen. I would much rather my kid make a mistake by blowing all their money on snacks at the age of twelve, than get out on his own, misuse a credit card, and run up thousands of dollars of debt in a matter of months and spend years paying it off.

Slow but Steady Progress

Don't expect your teen's money habits to just change overnight. It will be a gradual progression, with a few bumps along the way, no doubt! Think about it. How did you learn to drive? Did you just get a permit and then all of a sudden know everything? No, first you may have started in a parking lot. Next, you probably drove around the block or down the street. Then when you got comfortable, you were put in progressively harder situations. You didn't start your first drive at night, in the rain, on the interstate, in Atlanta, during rush hour.

Learning money management should be a progressive journey as well. We are slowly moving them along the path to more and more freedom and responsibility. If you don't teach your teen anything and just hope he figures money out on his own, the college campus with all of its newfound freedom and lack of parental controls could be compared to throwing a new driver out onto the Atlanta freeway.

Reflection Questions

1. Do I look at money as a blessing or a curse?

2. In the past, if my budget wasn't perfect, did I feel like a failure?

3. Do some items I buy my teen, like clothes, cause tension that could be eliminated by transferring control to them?

Chapter Eight
Let Them Fly!

It is not what you do for your children, but what you have taught them to do for themselves, that will make them successful human beings.

— Ann Landers

It is amazing to watch your teen grow up and become a responsible adult. One day they are toddling around, pounding on the bathroom door, asking a million questions, and the next they are ready to launch out on their own. The goal of every parent is to prepare them for life on their own. No one starts out on this parenting journey, holding a newborn at the hospital, thinking, "I'm going to do everything I can to screw up your life. If I'm lucky maybe you'll spend adulthood living in my basement." We all want our kids to do well, stand on their own two feet, and grow up to be successful, contributing members of society.

Letting go is a process. It shouldn't come all at once right after they graduate from high school. We need to be taking time throughout their childhood to gradually teach the skills we know they will need. It's not fair to let them spend their entire adolescence playing and having fun but not learning how to do anything. After they graduate we expect them to live on their own, but they often don't know how to cook, clean, handle money, or communicate with other adults.

When you start the plan, you need to commit ahead of time to be firm and not bail them out if they blow all their money and come begging for more. They are old enough to begin standing on their own two feet. That is not to say that they won't make some bad decisions. Remember our discussion about the prefrontal cortex? That doesn't mean they shouldn't have consequences; it just means that sometimes their decisions don't make sense. They will get better with more practice. Don't lecture when they mess up. Listen to their thoughts. Let them feel heard. You can say something like, "Oh wow. That's gonna hurt later." It's all right to commiserate with them, but you don't have to run in and fix the problem by giving them more money. Stepping in may make you feel good but will keep them from learning the lesson. Natural consequences have a wonderful way of teaching lessons that we never could have gotten across with all the lectures.

Every child will react differently when you introduce them to this plan. If you have multiple children, the first child will be the most likely to test the limits. The rest are watching to see what you do. Some kids will save every penny they can. Others will spend it all as soon as they get any money. The rest will be somewhere in the middle. However, once they get into the routine and are comfortable handling money, you will be amazed at how they mature.

Teach your teen how to negotiate. If she feels like her salary isn't enough, let her come up with proof and a well-thought-out proposal. You decide if your budget and your mind agrees with her. One of my girls who drives all the others to school came to me the other day and asked for more gasoline money. She talked about how many extra trips she was making. She was driving an extra trip every day to pick up her sister from sports practice. I listened, considered her request, and raised her gasoline amount.

Many adults have such a negative yucky feeling about money. Money is not evil. If we teach our teens how it works and help them understand money, they won't fear it. If they automatically give and save right off the top and know how to live on the rest, life won't be a struggle. In the past, I always struggled with guilt about spending money. Part of this guilt was because we were underemployed and had wrong mindsets regarding money. We also didn't really have sinking funds that we contributed to every month for things like clothes, Christmas, etc. If we can teach our children to give every dollar a place to go before they spend it, when they want to go buy that outfit, they can see there is $100 in the clothing fund and happily buy and enjoy it. They won't have the financial stress and worry about whether they just spent the rent or grocery money on a shirt.

Many people think they have an income problem. Some people do, but most of them don't. Every family earns different salaries, has a different number of people, and lives in a different area. However, the vast majority of them have the same complaint - we don't make enough money. How is that possible? If they had been taught the power of saving and giving first before they determined their lifestyle, it would not be such a widespread problem. The Internal Revenue Service discovered the power of this many years ago. Their payment comes out of your paycheck first. You don't ever think of that money as your own to use. You base your lifestyle around what's left after taxes.

Budgeting isn't so much about numbers. It's about awareness and consciously deciding what we are going to spend our money on rather than mindlessly spending. Your budget is not to control you. It is to assist you in being able to pay not only for your needs, but also your dreams. If you don't know how much you make and where it's going, you will make unwise decisions. You will waste your money on things that you halfway want and may have been willing to do without, if you had known they were keeping you from things that you really want.

Be your teen's money coach. If you haven't done well with money in the past, it's okay. Kids know parents aren't perfect, but they need to see you are working to change what needs improving. If you talk about the importance of financial management, but your finances are a mess, your actions will speak louder than your words. Let them see you reading books and listening to podcasts to improve both your knowledge and your life. Help them set up savings and investing accounts, get some books on finances, and listen to financial podcasts together.

Make sure your teen understands the power of starting early and saving consistently. Most people don't start saving for retirement until they are in their thirties. When you are young, it can seem like you have all the time in the world. "Retirement is so far off, I can get to it later." This delayed start causes several things to happen. First, your teen could potentially lose millions of dollars in compound interest by waiting ten or fifteen years to begin investing. Second, they design their lifestyle and budget to reflect their income before savings. Their entire paycheck will already be accounted for, and there will be no room for savings or emergencies.

Ideally, when your children are young, talk to them about saving for retirement and how they need to set aside 10 percent and pay themselves first. They will think this is just expected and everyone does it. They will not be spending everything they are making from the start. When they learn to set their lifestyle at an amount that comes after giving, retirement savings, and other savings, they can comfortably live without being stretched to the max.

In fact, they may even find themselves in the ranks of the ever growing FIRE movement - financially independent, retire early. People in this group save extreme amounts of money at the beginning of their careers when they are younger. As a result, they may be able to retire in their forties or fifties, years ahead of their peers. They can then devote the rest of their life to worthy causes and dreams, instead of being stuck on the treadmill of their debts and their lifestyle.

What happens if you don't teach your teens anything? Where will they learn it? Do you think they will learn it from their friends? I know young adult behavior. They want to look like they have it all together. They think everyone else has it figured out. The majority of them will not ask for financial help from their teachers or even their friends, who are probably also broke.

The Ball's in Your Court

So here we are at the end of our journey together. We started at the beginning talking about some of the mistakes Keith and I had made as young adults and how we were able to overcome our challenges. Then we discussed what money looks like for most people, and how we don't want our children to be financially normal. The next chapter we covered how learning new skills would transform not only our teen's competence, but also their confidence. Next, we talked about the importance of having financial goals and a plan for what you want your teen to learn. Finally, we discussed the practical steps that you could take to help your teen learn the lessons while they were still at home.

Imagine yourself ten or fifteen years in the future. Your teen went through high school using the money plan. Not only did the plan help you teach him how to handle money, but it also helped you become a better money manager. At his first job in high school, your teen started putting money into a 401(k) and already has a tidy little nest egg. At college graduation, he had no debt. He had committed to not getting student loans and did not get sucked into the credit card trap like so many college friends. When starting his career he prioritized planning his financial future. He and his growing family just bought a house. They don't experience the money stress that so many couples face because they are not living on the edge.

I am excited for you and your teen and what the future holds for you! I would love to hear how this book has helped you. Share your thoughts and goals with me at Rachel@RachelMurphyCoaching.com.

You don't have to get it perfect,
you just have to get it going.
— Jack Canfield

THE MONEY PLAN PATH

1. **WRITE OUT YOUR GOALS**
   If you don't know where you are going, how will you know when you get there? Have a plan.

2. **PICK YOUR CATEGORIES**
   Select a few categories that you can use to start your teen on the plan.

3. **DETERMINE CURRENT SPENDING**
   Calculate how much you are currently spending on those categories.

4. **DECIDE FAMILY GUIDELINES**
   What will be the rules for your family? Think them through.

5. **INTRODUCE PLAN**
   Schedule a family meeting to introduce the plan to your teen.

6. **SET UP BUDGETING APPS**
   Decide on a method to help your teen track their money.

7. **CELEBRATE!**
   Enjoy watching your teen become responsible!

Someone is sitting In the shade today because someone planted a tree a long time ago.

Warren Buffett

The Money Plan 2.0

Take Your Teen to the Next Level

Without ambition one starts nothing.
Without work one finishes nothing.
The prize will not be sent to you.
You have to win it.

—Ralph Waldo Emerson

Once your teen has been on the plan for a few years, you may want to go even deeper in preparation to launch them financially. When they turn eighteen, it might be a good time to take them off of the joint account with you and place them on their own account. This would be a great time to start paying them with a check, if you haven't already. They need to learn how to endorse a check and write their account number on the back so they can deposit it. This can also provide them with practice depositing it online and in person. If you want to go a step further beyond that, you can raise their salary, but require them to start paying rent and car insurance. This gets them into the habit of remembering to pay a monthly obligation. The more practice they get, the more prepared they will be.

Investing

When your teen starts thinking about getting a regular job or starting a business, begin planting seeds in their mind about the power of compound interest and investing. It can be fun to pull up an investing calculator and see what an impact time and amount invested have on the long-term results of savings. The website https://investor.gov has a good compound interest calculator. Input different numbers and let your teen see what a difference it would make if they started investing earlier. If they work at a company that has a 401(k) match, that would be a great place to begin investing. Not only is the money they contribute growing, but also so is the match that the employer contributes. Where else can you get free money like that? Bankrate has a 401(k) retirement calculator that will enable you to input how much you contribute, how much your employer will contribute and how much your money will grow because of that match.

If the employer doesn't have a 401(k) available or your teen is self-employed, they can set up a Roth IRA. A Roth IRA is funded with after-tax retirement contributions. This is awesome for a teen because the first $12,200 they earn is not taxed. Very few teens are going to be making more than that amount. If they make below the threshold, they are investing money into their retirement without any taxes taken out. This money also won't have any taxes taken out at withdrawal. Another benefit of a Roth is earnings may be withdrawn without penalty for college expenses, first-time purchase of a house, birth and adoption expenses, and certain medical expenses.

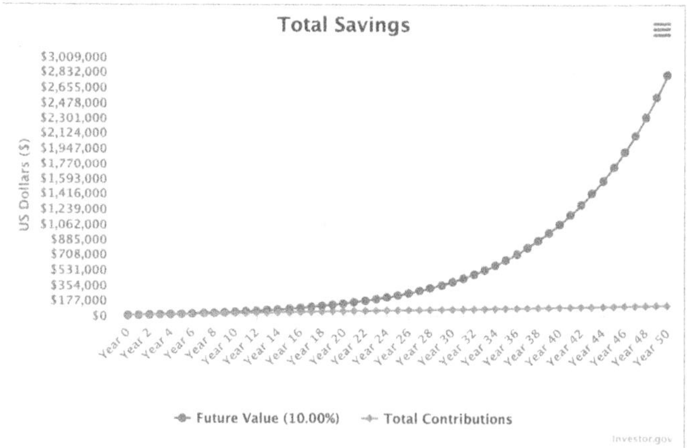

If you had a starting balance of $100 and deposited $200 a month at a 10% interest rate, after fifty years you would have contributed $120,100 of your own money. However, because of compounding interest, your total would be $2,805,119.55!

Credit Cards

Once your teen has mastered cash and has spent several years using a debit card, you may want to think about introducing a credit card. I know that some financial influencers believe that people should never have credit cards. I, however, know some people spend more money and have a more difficult time managing their finances when they use cash. Also, it can be very difficult to rent an apartment, get a mortgage or even buy a cell phone with no credit history. However, getting a credit card is not something that should be taken lightly. You need to discuss all the potential benefits and dangers with your teen.

This is personal finance - what works for one person may not work for another. When Keith and I were having financial struggles, we avoided credit cards for about ten years and then slowly reintroduced them into our lives. We have used them for many years since, pay them off every month, and never pay any interest.

Your teen needs to understand the difference between debit cards and credit cards. Debit cards take the money out of your account immediately upon purchase. Credit cards, on the other hand, allow you to borrow money from the card issuer to purchase items or receive cash advances. If the money is not repaid by the due date, the issuer will charge interest on the amount borrowed. With a credit card, it can be very easy to spend more than you have the ability to repay. For this reason, many people carry credit card balances. The teen must understand this tendency and keep careful records of purchases. If he ever has a month where he cannot pay the balance off, he needs to quit using the credit card and go back to cash or a debit card.

One of the big perks of a credit card is that it keeps someone from having to carry cash, especially while traveling. Credit cards offer more protection from fraud and make it easier to rent a car or reserve a hotel stay. If someone unauthorized were to use your debit card you may be liable, especially if the theft is not discovered quickly. Also with a debit card, even if the activity was determined to be fraudulent, refunding your money may take several weeks. Another credit card benefit is the ability to earn cash back and travel rewards from purchases. Many items bought on a credit card also have purchase protection. If certain goods or services were purchased that you felt were unsatisfactory or not fulfilled, it is possible to dispute the charges. Insurance may also cover travel or rental cars.

Along with the benefits, there are also disadvantages. The cardholder must be disciplined. It is easy to overspend because the money does not come directly out of the bank account at purchase. If the balance is not paid off every month, interest fees will be added to the balance. When a payment is not made on time, not only will there be late fees, but also a negative effect on the cardholder's credit report and credit score.

If your teen has been on the plan for several years and is doing well, I recommend that the last year of high school he be put on your credit card as an authorized user if you have a good credit history and score. This will enable him to start building a credit history. Make sure your card issuer doesn't charge to add authorized users. Your teen doesn't even have to use the card, if you feel he is not quite ready yet. Just having his name as an authorized user will begin to build his credit history.

If you do give him the card, I would keep a close eye on the account and make sure he is handling it responsibly. My teens use my card on which they are authorized users only to buy purchases for me, for example, if they are going to the store and I ask them to pick up groceries for the family. They cannot use this card for themselves because they are responsible for their own purchases.

Before your teen gets their own credit card, I would have a serious sit-down meeting to show how much more they are charged when carrying a balance. Many people have never sat down and looked at how much credit card interest is costing them. Pull up a credit card minimum payment calculator. (Bankrate has a good one.) Type in the cost of a big-ticket item, and let them see how much it will really cost only paying the minimums. Here is an example using the average credit card debt of $5,315 at the average interest rate of 16.15 percent.

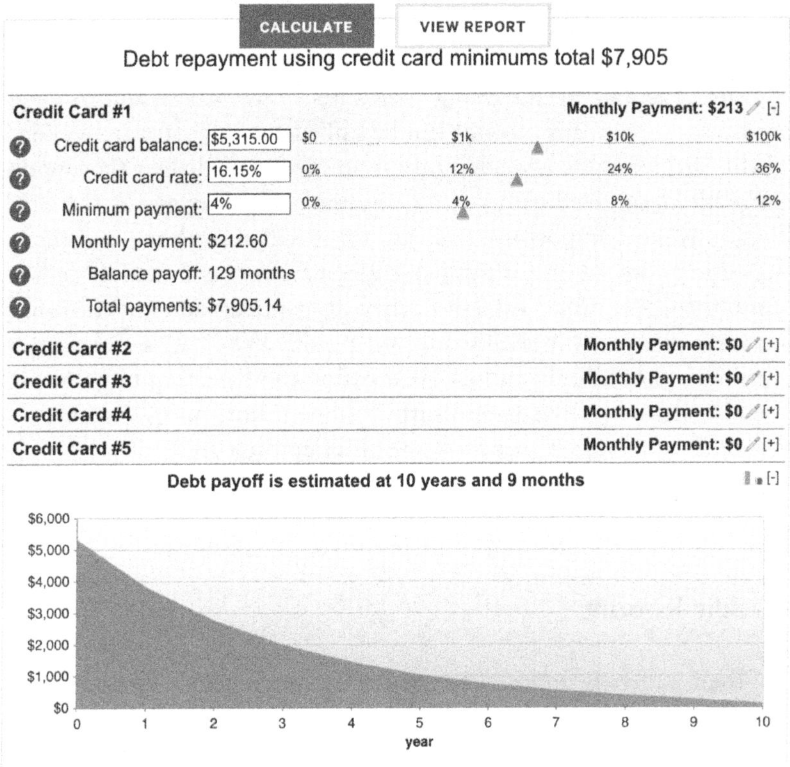

Credit cards also offer something called a cash advance. A cash advance looks like a debit card withdrawal from your ATM. It sounds wonderful, but don't ever do it. Not only will the lender charge a higher interest rate than a normal credit card purchase, but there is no grace period. Interest will be charged starting from the date the cash was withdrawn. There is also a cash advance fee of three to five percent of the amount borrowed. In addition, there are ATM or bank fees for withdrawing the money. The convenience of borrowing the money is not worth what it will cost. When we were younger and having financial trouble, we used cash advances a few times. It's a horrible cycle in which to get stuck. You need to learn how to manage money now to prevent these unnecessary expenses and stress. If you have an emergency fund, you should never need a cash advance.

Once your teen turns eighteen and has a regular job, you can discuss applying for their own credit card. They probably won't be able to get a card with great rewards and perks, but they may be able to get one with some type of rewards. There is no single best card for everyone.

Compare several and look for the one that best fits your needs. Look for a card with no annual fee. Starting out, your teen will probably need to look for a student or secured credit card.

I love the You Need a Budget software for the way it handles credit cards. The credit card account can be linked to your software. When a credit card purchase is made, you can immediately deduct the amount from the designated category. For example, if I buy gas at the Shell station, when I import my transactions it will show Shell and then a deduction coming out of the fuel category. Every transaction deducts from the appropriate category when it happens and moves into a separate pile just for the credit card payoff. When it is time to pay the credit card bill, the money is all sitting there waiting to go toward the bill. This way there are no surprises about how much you spent. It would also be great if your teen would set up their credit card bill to be paid automatically in full on or before the due date.

Credit Report

There are two important terms when it comes to credit - credit report and credit score. Your credit report is a record of your financial history. It is updated every month or so. The payments that normally show on your credit report are auto loans, mortgages, student loans, and credit cards. Other items, such as your rent, insurance, utilities, and medical bills may show up on your report if paid late. These bills along with collections, bankruptcies, charge-offs, and foreclosures will show up and affect your report negatively. The accounts are listed showing the age of each account and how much owed. The report also lists any inquires that have been made on your credit. Your credit report will determine your credit score.

After your teen has had a credit card for several months, show him how to pull a credit report. There are three main credit reporting agencies—Equifax, Experian, and Transunion. Anyone is allowed one free credit report from all three bureaus every twelve months at https://annualcreditreport.com. Your teen could check all three agencies at once, but I prefer to pull a report from one of the agencies every four months. Have your teen set a reminder in his calendar to check his credit report.

Credit Score

One of the main reasons to have a credit card is to start building a credit score, also known as your FICO score. This is a number between 300 and 850 that tells lenders how likely you are to pay your bills on time. To have a score, a person must have had at least one account for the last six months that was reported to the credit agencies. The higher the score, the less of a risk to the lender. For that reason, people with higher scores receive better interest rates on mortgages and loans.

A credit score is determined by the following factors: payment history (35%), amounts owed (30%), length of credit history (15%), credit mix (10%), and new credit (10%). When just starting out, either because of age or lack of credit history, your teen must be even more diligent with their credit. The report averages all credit accounts. If a person only has one or two accounts, those accounts are going to count for more. An older adult may have several credit cards, a mortgage, and a student loan. If that person paid late on one of those bills months ago, it won't be as detrimental because there are more accounts and more history to average.

1. *Payment history* is the most important factor. This is determined by whether you pay your bills on time. You must pay your bills and pay them on time!

2. The next most important factor is *amount owed.* It is also called the credit utilization ratio. Lenders want to know how much available credit is being used. Using all available credit, even if the bill is paid off every month, makes a person look like a higher risk. You don't want to appear like you are living above your means to repay. The goal is to owe less than thirty percent of your available credit.

   For example, if your teen has one credit card with a $1,000 limit, she needs to keep the balance below $300. The amount is calculated by looking at all available credit. For example, if a person had three cards with a total available credit of $5,000, they should not let the total of all the balances exceed $1,500.

3. The third factor is length of *credit history.* The longer the credit history, the better it looks. Since your teen is just starting out, there really is no getting around it. Their credit history just won't be very long. We already discussed one thing you can do. If you have good credit, you can put your teen on one of your cards as an authorized user, and that will favorably influence their credit report and score. Make sure your card issuer reports authorized users to the credit agencies.

4. The next factor is *credit mix.* This shows the lenders what types of accounts (installment or revolving) and how many of them you have. *Installment accounts* are accounts like mortgages and car loans where a person pays a fixed amount monthly. *Revolving accounts* are credit accounts that let you borrow money and pay it back over time. Lenders want to see that a person can maintain good credit across different types of debt. This factor is not that important, so I wouldn't focus too much on getting more credit.

5. The final factor is *new credit.* This component considers any new credit just received as well as new credit applications. A person should be careful not to apply for a bunch of loans or credit cards at the same time. Doing this makes someone appear like they are preparing to take on a bunch of debt. I know all those stores in the mall are offering 10 percent off for applying; just because you can doesn't mean you should!

Many lenders look at both the credit report and credit score to determine if they will extend a loan and how much interest will be charged. Excellent credit scores will get a better interest rate. This could potentially save thousands of dollars over the life of the loan. Sometimes when applying for a job the company will check your credit report, especially if the job involves handling money. They want to see if you are responsible or if you are having any financial difficulties which increase the risk for fraud or theft.

There is another credit score that is becoming more popular called the VantageScore. The VantageScore was created by the three major credit bureaus (Equifax, Experian, and TransUnion) as an alternative to the FICO. Lenders for many years have mainly used the FICO, but they are beginning to pay more attention to the VantageScore. This is great news because people who had trouble getting a score in the past because of limited credit history, such as young adults, find it easier to get a VantageScore. With a FICO score you need at least six months of credit history compared to only a month or two with VantageScore.

The two scoring agencies use much of the same data to calculate your score, but calculate the numbers a little differently. It doesn't really matter which one you use, they both are reporting your credit history and worthiness. One will not report a low score, while the other reports a high score. Just pick one. Many credit cards offer free credit score reporting. With some cards, such as Capital One and Discover, you do not even have to be a customer. You can also obtain a free score through personal financial sites like CreditKarma and NerdWallet.

CREDIT SCORE FACTORS

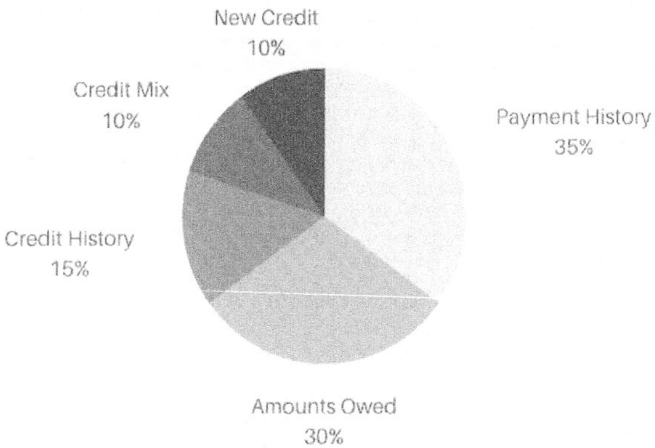

Six months after your teen has begun to use her credit card, she should check her credit score.

- Exceptional 800 to 850
- Very Good 740 to 799
- Good 670 to 739
- Fair 580 to 669

If your teen has been on the plan for a few years and become adept at budgeting, investing, and being the master of telling their money where to go, they will be miles ahead of almost every adult in the country. Most people don't have a clue where their money goes every month, nor know the steps they need to take to learn. They may have a vague idea of what they want out of life, but have never sat down and really thought about what they want and made a plan of how to achieve it.

If you've taken the time to implement the money plan your teen holds in their power the ability to succeed financially. Your intentional teaching and conversations have given them one of the greatest gifts possible. I can't wait to hear where life takes them. Drop me a note and let me know.

Action Steps

1. If your teen has a job, help them set up a 401(k) or Roth IRA. (30 minutes)

2. Help your teen check their credit report. (20 minutes)

3. Help your teen check their credit score. (10 minutes)

Tips for Those with Younger Children

I know some of you may have picked up this book and your kids aren't yet in middle school or high school. That's awesome. Like I said earlier, I learned of this idea when I only had one child who was a preschooler. I just kept the information in the back of my head, and when the time was right, I created the money plan. I do have some ideas that you can do now to help your younger children start understanding the value of money.

Start having money conversations early. Talk to your children about needs versus wants and how they need to manage money wisely. Explain to your children that Christmas and vacations are not emergencies. These events happen every year, so plan accordingly by setting aside money in advance.

Most children can begin learning these principles at a young age. One of my friends took her seven kids to the farmers' market one weekend. Her children are all seventh grade and younger. Before they left the house, she told them, "We are only going to buy vegetables. Don't ask for other stuff." Farmers' markets can be tempting environments. The produce is so pretty and colorful. The baked goods look so yummy, and there are so many cool handmade products to purchase.

They came upon a vendor selling honey. On the table were pint Mason jars full of delicious honey lemonade that cost six dollars each. Her kids love lemonade. They looked at Mom with pleading eyes. She said, "I'm not buying lemonade, but you guys have your own money. Maybe you can each put in a little and buy one together." So, after a bit of discussion, some of her kids decided to put their money together and buy one. She said that they took tiny sips. They savored it, and that lemonade lasted most of the day.

Those kids learned a great lesson. Mom could have said, "We are not getting any lemonade; it's not in the budget." Mom could have bought everyone a lemonade, totally blowing the budget. Instead, she let them have control. They thought it out, made a decision, and appreciated the lemonade even more.

Let them start little businesses and make their own money. There are so many businesses kids can do these days to earn money. Don't be too overbearing about this. They are kids, and wanting to make a little money shouldn't shackle them to years of commitment. I'm not saying let them change businesses every week, but let them try things for a season and then go on to something else.

Don't pay them extreme amounts to do extra chores around the house. I may swing too far to the other end on this one, but I want self-employment or a job to be easier on my kids than what they had to do at home and not the other way around.

Don't use the, "We can't afford it," reason for not buying stuff. Instead, say, "We are choosing not to spend our money on that." Otherwise, the child will always feel like they are poor and the solution is more money.

Teach them the importance of giving. If you are even reading this book or thinking about this subject, you are one of the most fortunate people in the world. You don't have to worry about where your next meal is coming from or if you are going to be able to find clean water to drink tomorrow. Often, though, we forget and compare ourselves to others around us. We feel like we deserve more and we don't have enough.

When a person gives, it changes their perspective. They realize that they don't have to hold so tightly to possessions. Giving is a reminder that you have enough and calms down the monster of selfishness. I try not to think of money in my possession as mine, but rather as a resource that is placed in my possession while I am here on earth that I need to manage well to help others and take care of my family. This mindset helps prevent freaking out when financial challenges happen.

One of the best ways to teach kids about generosity and thankfulness is to expose them to others that may be going through hard times or may not have as much as they do. Volunteer together to help others that are less fortunate. An experience serving meals at a homeless shelter or even visiting a third-world country, if possible, can change a person's perspective like no book can. Let them see you giving and let them experience the joy of giving too.

Start out from the beginning having an expectation of saving and giving a portion of any money they earn. If saving and giving is normal from the beginning, then it won't be a disappointment to them when they are older and you tell them that they need to start saving part of their paycheck. They have already been saving and it has become a habit.

I really want to do this plan, but . . .

We are so strapped financially; we don't have the money to do this.

I understand being in extreme financial shape. The car we bought when we were digging out of debt was a $1,500 green Saturn with peeling paint. It was a manual transmission, which I didn't know how to drive. It was what we could afford, so that's what we bought. In order to get anywhere, I had to learn how to drive a stick shift. The next vehicle was a GMC Safari van which had the air conditioner break not too long after we bought it. We lived pretty far out of town, so for years we would freeze water bottles to stick on our laps to help cool us down while riding in the Florida heat. I remember spending $1.07 on entertainment for the month with one Redbox movie. I understand money being tight. If you are in that situation, what is your plan? Is it a temporary situation? What are the steps you are going to take to improve your income - job advancement, career change, or a side business?

Don't give up! You can still teach these principles to your teen. Could you start a side business with your teen and let him have a percentage of the profits for his spending plan? Could your teen get a job, and you teach him how to make a spending plan with his income? I doubt your teens are hungry and running around naked. Where do they get their clothes? If you get them from the thrift store, you can still have a clothing budget based on thrift store prices. Maybe they can help you with the grocery budget. Discuss with them how much money you have for food and get them to help you figure out what recipes to prepare and how to make the money last the month.

I know sometimes parents are ashamed and don't want their kids to know how tight money is, but teens understand more than we think they do. Making your teen part of the team may give them a better understanding of how stretched the budget is and enable them to be part of the solution. I've heard many stories of parents who want to give their kids everything (that's natural) but end up putting themselves in extreme credit card debt and stress. However, if the teen had known the full picture, they might not have cared about what brand of clothing they got.

I am divorced, and my ex won't go along with the plan.

Let me be clear, I am no therapist. If you have a good relationship with your ex, could you sit down together and have a conversation? If your marriage involved financial challenges, you can discuss how you don't want your child to go through similar money struggles as an adult. Maybe you could loan your ex this book and come up with a plan together.

If you have an unwilling ex, then you can only control what goes on in your own house. Do your best to have regular money conversations with your teen, and just implement what you can. Don't beat yourself up; any progress is better than none.

My own finances are in such a mess; I don't know how to begin teaching my teen.

You are taking the first step! That is huge! You are willing to admit you need to learn. Begin setting some personal goals for yourself and your money. Start reading some books and listening to some podcasts and planning how you are going to change your own financial life. While you are doing that, you may just want to do only one or two categories with your teen. Be honest with your teen about how you haven't been proactive enough about your finances and want to start changing your life. Talk to them about how you want to help them change their life too. Start learning and sharing what you learn with them. This is exciting! You can do it! I am rooting for you!

Suggested Resources

Books

A Teenager's Guide to Investing in the Stock Market by Luke Villermin
Debt-Proof Living by Mary Hunt
Get Good with Money by Tiffany Aliche
How to Adult: Personal Finance for the Real World by Jake Cousineau
Make Your Kid a Money Genius (Even If You're Not) by Beth Kobliner
Raising Financially Confident Kids by Mary Hunt
The Automatic Millionaire by David Bach
The Latte Factor by David Bach
The Richest Man in Babylon by George S. Clason
MONEY SMARTS: What Students Want, Graduates Need, and Parents Wish to Know About Money by Nathan Nguyen
Set For Life by Scott Trench
Teach Your Child to Fish by Holly Reid (younger children)

Software

EveryDollar
Goodbudget
You Need a Budget
Qube

Podcasts

Bigger Pockets Money
His and Her Money
Marriage, Kids and Money
Redefining Wealth

Miscellaneous

Free annual credit report https://annualcreditreport.com
Free credit score https://creditkarma.com
Investing calculator https://investor.gov
Credit card minimum payment calculator
https://bankrate.com/calculators/credit-cards/credit-card-minimum-payment

All forms are available at https://rachelmurphycoaching.com/book-resource

Hi friend,

Thank you so much for purchasing my book, *I Am Not Your ATM: A Practical Plan for Teaching Your Teen to Manage Money.* I know that you are very busy and could have done many other things. Thank you so much for sharing your time with me.

I hope that you received value from reading this book that will help you as you guide the teenagers in your life. If so, I would love to hear from you and would greatly appreciate it if you could post a review on Amazon. Your feedback will not only help me, but also other parents who could benefit as they teach their teens about money.

Thank you so much! Your input is very important. I wish you all the best in your parenting journey!

Rachel

Appendix

Current Spending Checklist

- [ ] Spending money
- [ ] Treats/Snacks
- [ ] Birthday gifts for friends/family
- [ ] Church or youth activities
- [ ] Christmas gifts for friends/family/teachers
- [ ] School lunches
- [ ] Food at school events/sporting events
- [ ] Meals out
- [ ] Clothes/shoes
- [ ] School supplies
- [ ] Tolietries
- [ ] Makeup
- [ ] Haircuts
- [ ] Gasoline
- [ ] Cellphone
- [ ] Senior Trip
- [ ]

Recommended Categories by Grade

5th Grade
Charity
Savings
Spending money
Treats/snacks

6th Grade
Charity
Savings
Spending money
Treats/snacks
Birthday gifts for friends/family
Church or youth activities

7th Grade
Charity
Savings
Spending money
Treats/snacks
Birthday gifts for friends/family
Church or youth activities
Christmas gifts for friends/family
School lunches

Recommended Categories by Grade

8th Grade

Charity
Savings
Spending money
Treats/snacks
Birthday gifts for friends/family
Church or youth activities
Christmas gifts for friends/family
School lunches
Food at school events/sporting events
Meals out

9th Grade

Charity
Savings
Spending money
Treats/snacks
Birthday gifts for friends/family
Church or youth activities
Christmas gifts for friends/family
School lunches
Food at school events/sporting events
Meals out
Clothes/shoes
School supplies
Makeup/toiletries

Recommended Categories by Grade

10th Grade
Charity
Savings
Spending money
Treats/snacks
Birthday gifts for friends/family
Church or youth activities
Christmas gifts for friends/family
School lunches
Food at school events/sporting events
Meals out
Clothes/shoes
School supplies
Makeup/toiletries
Haircuts

Recommended Categories by Grade

11th Grade
Charity
Savings
Spending money
Treats/snacks
Birthday gifts for friends/family
Church or youth activities
Christmas gifts for friends/family
School lunches
Food at school events/sporting events
Meals out
Clothes/shoes
School supplies
Makeup/toiletries
Haircuts
Homecoming/prom
Gasoline

Recommended Categories by Grade

12th Grade
Charity
Savings
Spending money
Treats/snacks
Birthday gifts for friends/family
Church or youth activities
Christmas gifts for friends/family
School lunches
Food at school events/sporting events
Meals out
Clothes/shoes
School supplies
Makeup/toiletries
Haircuts
Homecoming/prom
Gasoline
Cellphone
Senior Trip

CATEGORIES FOR MATTHEW

	CATEGORY	AMOUNT
1.	CHARITY	$4
2.	SAVINGS	$4
3.	SPENDING MONEY	$20
4.	SNACKS	$12
5.		
6.		
7.		
8.		
9.		
10.		
TOTAL		$40

CATEGORIES FOR ____________

CATEGORY	AMOUNT
1.	
2.	
3.	
4.	
5.	
6.	
7.	
8.	
9.	
10.	
TOTAL	

Spending TRACKER

MONTH

May

DATE	DESCRIPTION	AMOUNT
2/2	Snacks at the gas station	$3.80
2/5	Jeans	$29
2/6	Basketball game entry	$4
2/6	BB game concessions	$7
2/8	Chipolte	$10
2/12	Haircut	$20
2/17	Trampoline park	$15
2/17	Froyo	$6

Spending TRACKER

MONTH

DATE	DESCRIPTION	AMOUNT

GUIDELINES TO CONSIDER

- What age/grade will we start the plan? When will we end the plan?
- Will we require savings? What percent?
- Will we require giving? What percent?
- Will we allow the use of debit cards?
- Will we allow the use of credit cards?
- Will we have any restrictions on what they can buy?
- Will chores be a part of our plan?
- Will we contribute towards the purchase of their first car? Will we give a set amount or match up to a certain amount?
- How will our plan change when they get a job?

MY MONEY PLAN

NAME: ANDREW		DATE: SEPT 2022
MONTHLY SALARY: $130	SAVINGS GOAL: CAR	
CATEGORY	**SUGGESTED AMOUNT**	**PLANNED AMOUNT**
CHARITY	$13	$13
SAVINGS	$13	$13
FOOD OUT	$24	$19
HAIRCUTS	$10	$10
CLOTHES	$50	$60
SPORTS EVENTS	$20	$15

Every month on the 1st, $ __$13__ will be deposited into your savings account and $__$117__ will be deposited into your checking account for a total of $____$130___.

Reminder: Your planned amount doesn't have to stay the same all year. It Is just to give you a starting point.

MY MONEY PLAN

NAME:		DATE:
MONTHLY SALARY:	SAVINGS GOAL:	

CATEGORY	SUGGESTED AMOUNT	PLANNED AMOUNT

Every month on the 1st, $ _________ will be deposited into your savings account. These categories_________________________ _____________________will be given in cash for a total of $________.

Reminder: Your planned amount doesn't have to stay the same all year. It Is just to give you a starting point.

MY MONEY PLAN

NAME: DATE:

MONTHLY SALARY: SAVINGS GOAL:

CATEGORY	SUGGESTED AMOUNT	PLANNED AMOUNT

Every month on the 1st, $ _________ will be deposited into your savings account and $_________ will be deposited into your checking account for a total of $_____________.

Reminder: Your planned amount doesn't have to stay the same all year. It Is just to give you a starting point.

Our Financial Agreement

On this day of ______________________, 20__ ______________________ is taking the first steps towards becoming an adult and handling money wisely. We, your parents, love you and want the best for you. One of the greatest skills we can teach you is how to handle money and so today we are agreeing to do our part to help you learn these skills.

Every month, on the first of the month, you will receive a salary of $________. This salary is to be used to pay for your expenses for the month. For this year, the categories you are responsible for are the following:____.

From this money you are also responsible for giving ten percent to a needy cause and saving ten percent for a long term goal. If unexpected expenses arise in one of those categories, we will discuss and come up with a solution. You are still expected to help around the house
and may suffer the consequences of a fine if you refuse.

____

Dad's Signature

____

Mom's Signature

____

Teen's Signature

MONTHLY BUDGET

MONTH OF SEPTEMBER

INCOME	BUDGETED	ACTUAL	DIFF.	NOTES
SALARY	$80	$80		
WAGES	$40	$40		BABYSITTING
CASH GIFTS	$30	$30		BIRTHDAY
OTHER				
TOTAL INCOME	$150	$150		

EXPENSES	BUDGETED	ACTUAL	DIFF.	NOTES
CHARITY	$15	$15		
SAVINGS	$30	$30		
CLOTHING	$60	$65	$-5	
TOILETRIES	$20	$20		
BLOW MONEY	$25	$20	$+5	MOVED TO CLOTHES
TOTAL EXPENSES	**$150**	**$150**		

Income minus expenses equals zero.

A budget is telling your money where to go, instead of wondering where It went. - John Maxwell

MONTHLY BUDGET

MONTH OF

INCOME	BUDGETED	ACTUAL	DIFF.	NOTES
SALARY				
WAGES				
CASH GIFTS				
OTHER				
TOTAL INCOME				

EXPENSES	BUDGETED	ACTUAL	DIFF.	NOTES
TOTAL EXPENSES				

Income minus expenses equals zero.

A budget is telling your money where to go, instead of wondering where It went. - John Maxwell

Acknowledgments

To God who has continually lead me to a deeper and deeper understanding of His love and my worth in Him, who carried us through, in spite of our stupid mistakes and allowed our biggest mess become a message to help others.

To Keith who probably worked on this book as many hours as I did. Apparently we are perfect for each other. No one else could put up with us and our crazy, non-stop "I have an idea." Thank you for always being willing to let me chase my dreams and help me get them. I love you.

To Ashton, Rebecca, Jenna, Hudson, and Eric – it's crazy being a Murphy kid. I know that you have been subjected to some of the wildest adventures. I hope those adventures have left you with great memories and not future therapy sessions. You all are my greatest treasure.

To my parents and in-laws – who were great examples of wise money managers, even if we didn't totally get the lessons.

To my business coach Nicole Walters – Thank you for believing in my abilities long before I did and for giving me kicks in the pants when I needed them.

To Nancy O'Brien – Thank you for all the time you spent reading my rough drafts and editing them for me. Your and Jack's encouragement and belief in me and my family have been priceless!

To Alyson Hughes, Bonnie Piatt, Nancy O'Brien, Brittany Bowman, Donna Ongalo, Denise Black, Honoray Joseph and Melly J – Thank you guys for all of your encouragement during this book writing process! It was so great having a team covering and encouraging me.

To Honoray Joseph - I don't think you knew what you were getting into when you agreed to design the book cover. Thank you for your patience with all my changes.

To all of my friends in my community (and some strangers) who let me pick their brains about their childhoods and how they were raised to think about money, thank you for your honesty and transparency. It was your input and thoughts that helped me write this book.

There were so many people who encourage me through this process – way too many to name! Your words of faith and belief in what I was doing have meant the world to me!

My money strategies have developed as a combination of all the knowledge from the financial experts that I have learned from over the years. I am so grateful for all the collective wisdom that I have learned from them. I don't think that I agree totally with everything any single one of them says. But there are concepts from each of them that I have really embraced and used to change my life over the years. That's what makes it personal finance.

Finance is a topic whose basics have never changed over thousands of years and if I can figure it out, you too can master those basics. I am always learning new things and getting better. When I look back and see how far my family has come, from living in one of the worst neighborhoods in our town and driving a paint chipped $1,500 car to living in a house that I never would have dreamed possible and most of all, not having the constant money stress. I am amazed and grateful. Don't fear change. An amazing life could be just around the corner. You wouldn't want to miss it!

End Notes

Chapter Two

1. Jon Simpson, "Finding Brand Success in the Digital World," August 25, 2017, https://forbes.com/sites/forbesagencycouncil/2017/08/25/finding-brand-success-in-the-digital-world/?sh=64a843aa626e.

2. Louis DeNicola, "Credit Card Use in College after the CARD Act," May 1, 2017, https://www.clearpoint.org/blog/credit-card-use-college-card-act/.

3. Dan Zapp, "2019 Money Matters on Campus," February 19, 2020, https://everfi.com/white-papers/financial-education/2019-money-matters-report/.

4. "Ally Bank Survey Shows Recent Grads Give Themselves a 'C Minus' in Personal Finance," Ally Financial, June 10, 2019, https://media.ally.com/2019-06-10-Ally-Bank-Survey-Shows-Recent-Grads-Give-Themselves-a-C-minus-in-Personal-Finance.

5. "2019 Majoring in Money Report," Sallie Mae and Ipsos, accessed May 30, 2021, https://www.salliemae.com/assets/about/who_we_are/Majoring-In-Money-Report-2019.pdf.

6. Mark Kantrowitz, "Student Loan Debt Statistics," July 23, 2020, https://www.savingforcollege.com/article/student-loan-statistics#:~:-text=More%than%20two%2Dthirds%20of,%2429%2C900%20in%20student%20loan%20debt.&text=These%2C%20and%20other%20student%20loan,expert%20on%20student%20loan%20debt.

7. "Survey: 65% of Americans Have No Idea How Much They Spent Last Month," Mint, last modified December 11, 2020, https://mint.intuit.com/blog/budgeting/spending-knowledge-survey.

8. Stefan Lembo Stolba, "Experian 2020 Consumer Credit Review," January 4, 2021, https://www.experian.com/blogs/ask-experian/consumer-credit-review/.

9. Jeff Ostrowski, "Survey: Fewer than 4 in 10 Americans Could Pay

a Surprise $1,000 Bill from Savings," January 11, 2021, https://www.bankrate.com/banking/savings/financial-security-january-2021/#:~:-text=Underscoring%20the%20shaky%20finances%20of,visit%20by%20tapping%20into%20savings.

10. "Money Ruining Marriages in America: a Ramsey Solutions Study," Ramsey Solutions, February 7, 2018, https://www.ramseysolutions.com/company/newsroom/releases/money-ruining-marriages-in-america.

11. "Money Causes the Most Stress for Couples," Ally, June 12, 2018, https://theharrispoll.com/money-causes-the-most-stress-for-couples-according-to-new-ally-survey/.

12. Christy Bieber, "The Average Cost of Divorce in 2020," November 16, 2020. https://www.fool.com/the-ascent/research/average-cost-of-divorce/.

13. Bankrate, Credit Card Minimum Payment Calculator, https://www.bankrate.com/calculators/credit-cards/credit-card-minimum-payment.aspx, accessed June 5, 2021.

14. U.S. Securities and Exchange Commission, Compound Interest Calculator, https://www.investor.gov/financial-tools-calculators/calculators/compound-interest-calculator, accessed June 5, 2021.

Chapter Three

1. Burchard, Brendon. "Episode 113: Become a Master in Any Field." The Brendon Show. Podcast audio, March 12, 2020. https://podcasts.apple.com/us/podcast/the-brendon-show/id821746377?i=1000468201096.

2. Dweck, Carol. Mindset: The New Psychology of Success. New York: 2011.

3. Jeannie Burlowski, telephone conversation with author, July 6, 2021.

Chapter Four

1. "BECU Survey Discovers Majority of Parents Aren't Talking with Kids about Money," BECU, October 3, 2019, https://www.prnewswire.com/news-releases/becu-survey-discovers-majority-of-parents-arent-talking-with-kids-about-money-300930307.html.

2. "Survey of the States 2020," Council for Economic Education, February 5, 2020, https://www.councilforeconed.org/survey-of-the-states-2020/.

3. Woods, Geoff, host. "Episode 275: Decide Your Habits; Decide Your Future." Interview with Gary Keller. The ONE Thing. Podcast audio, December 14, 2020. https://podcasts.apple.com/us/podcast/the-one-thing-with-geoff-woods/id1191482456?i=1000502329080.

Chapter Five

1. "Parents are Likely to Pass Down Good and Bad Financial Habit to Their Kids," T. Rowe Price, March 23, 2017, https://www.troweprice.com/corporate/us/en/press/t--rowe-price--parents-are-likely-to-pass-down-good-and-bad-fina0.html.

2. "Taking Stock with Teens Survey," Piper Sandler Investment Research, October 6, 2020, http://www.pipersandler.com/private/pdf/TSWTs_Fall_2020_Full_Report.pdf.

Chapter Seven

1. Clear, James. Atomic Habits: An Easy & Proven Way to Build Good Habits & Break Bad Ones. New York: 2018.

About the Author

Rachel Murphy has worked with young people for almost twenty-five years as a youth director, a foster parent, a mentor to young adults, and is a mom to five children (ages 8-24). Through the years she became aware of how many teens are lacking easily taught life skills that would help them as they launch out on their own. Her family started Raising Confident Teens to help teach life and leadership skills to teens and their parents. She is the main host of the Raising Confident Teens podcast, and her three teens take turns co-hosting. Rachel is also the moderator over at the Raising Confident Teens Community on Facebook, a community designed to support and empower parents as they navigate preparing their teens for adulthood.

Rachel lives on the Gulf Coast of Florida with her husband, Keith, their four children still at home, and a crazy dog named Bear. In this season of her life, you will find her most evenings at one of her kid's games or working on a podcast. Two of her favorite things are sitting down with someone to listen to their story and drinking sweet tea. If she can do both at the same time, it's a bonus. In her free time (what free time?), she likes to build furniture. You can find her online at RachelMurphyCoaching.com and on the Raising Confident Teens podcast.

Made in the USA
Coppell, TX
01 April 2022

75888120R00069